AF480906

Conversations of the Past

UTTARA VAID

ISBN
Paperback 979-8-89322-710-9
Hardcase 979-8-89777-680-1

Foreword

This is a work of introspection and meticulous research, all of it owing to a seemingly innocuous post on WhatsApp sent to me by one of my good friends referencing a small excerpt by a well-known speaker in Hindi literature, Mr. Kumar Vishwas. Very emphatically, Mr. Vishwas made out a case of how the entire Uttar Kand in Ramayan, an appendage to the main epic, had never happened but was later added to Valmiki's original Ramayan. The real purpose behind this may never be unravelled, but it could have been done in the reign of foreign rulers, the Mughals and the British to completely discredit our Gods and shake the foundations of Sanatan Dharma and our faith in our Hindu religion and thus facilitate easy conversions and easier conquer of our fertile lands.

I still remember the lasting impact his words had on me exhorting his audience not to believe without verifying all the facts. The fact remains that, the most incriminating allegation against Ram that he abandoned his unimpeachable wife Sita when she was pregnant and left her to her own devices in a forest; has very little proof it having actually happened! Valmiki's Ramayan ends at coronation and if indeed Sita stayed in the Valmiki Ashram and delivered and brought up both Luv and Kush in his Ashram, why wouldn't Valmiki add that to his original Ramayan? In fact, all the three main episodes of Uttar Kand are so uncharacteristic of Ram and seem so contrived to suit vested interests that they defy all logic and this is where Mr. Vishwas[1] ended with a poignant and thought provoking question:

---

1   Refer to Dr. Kumar Vishwas's recordings on You Tube expostulating his views on Uttar Kand -Ramayan, Sita's exile…

"The problem lies not with the addition of such defamatory and vilifying addition to our sacred literature; the problem lies in the fact that Hindus believe this! Should somebody utter even the slightest slanderous matter against our near and dear ones, will we accept it without proof or an explanation? Then, why are we so ready to accept such vilification against our Gods?"

This was an epiphany for me and I cannot imagine for how many women of my age, when as impressionable young girls we were taught that our God actually abandoned his wife because a Dhobi uttered some irresponsible remarks! As independent young girls carving out their personal and professional identities in this world, a man or God like that could never be worshipped, and after hearing this, I suddenly felt so small, so ashamed of myself – the problem lay with me, why was I ready to believe such drivel against my God? It then occurred to me that because Ram was God, he could survive such vilification for centuries and still continue to be worshipped!

And then, as I started to read more and more, delved into research and discovered many hidden gems, I was inspired; these would lend themselves so beautifully to poetry rather than prose. Soon, I had an entire series of thirty plus sonnets titled "Conversations of the Past" in which each sonnet captures one random conversation from our ancient history such as the Ramayan, Mahabharat, Shiv Puran, and is carefully chosen to shine a spotlight on an incident, a conversation, a character that does not form a part of the oft-repeated narrative of the epic. Since these are random conversations, each of these have been prefaced with a prologue that sets a context and recreates the background of the conversations to the uninitiated reader. The conversations may be a dialogue, a soliloquy, a reflection, or a plea from the poet to the protagonist from the past, (Indeed my first sonnet is a plea from a devotee to the God Himself), what they bring to the reader is a precious nugget from the past which has lain buried like hidden treasure, to be researched and discovered now.

The prologue also serves to explain certain nuances so that the reader's appreciation of even the little-known instances or incidents, integral to the entire poem, are heightened considerably, thus resulting in a more complete immersive experience. Therefore, the prologue and the poem must be read together to enjoy them thoroughly.

Needless to say, each sonnet ends with a beautiful couplet that skilfully weaves the present into our ancient past and reminds the reader that despite the humongous passage of time, mankind may still be facing the same dilemmas today, that somethings never change, and age-old wisdom is as relevant today as it was eons ago when times were different.

This also necessitates a disclaimer – if there is no agreement on whether Uttar Kand in Ramayan actually happened, which is fundamental to the topic, it is quite likely that many of my readers may be at variance with some of the topics, contents, or episodes of this collection. My research has been quite broad, ranging from popular TV serials, published material on the public domain, and needless to say, I have also picked up topics that piqued my poetic curiosity and imagination. So, rather than getting into controversies that this never happened (for example, Ram never wrote a letter to Kaikeyi!) I would urge the readers to read it purely for the sake of enjoyment and enlightenment if they feel so. They are a faithful rendition of many hidden anecdotes and because they have been *hidden,* it is quite likely that the reader may have discovered them only now through this volume (for example, to many readers in my private circulation, the fact that Ram actually had a sister came as a surprise!) but a simple Google search will reveal that Shanta actually did exist and is mentioned quite extensively in many research sources!

My sincere appeal to all my readers is to set yourself up to explore themes and areas you have never been to before and enjoy this sojourn into uncharted territory!

This is where I would also like to thank these handful few people who have been so encouraging in this journey of mine and actually demanded that I publish them for a larger audience; thanks all, without you all this publication would probably have never happened!

Mr. Parag Kamani, my sisters, Soni and Sangeeta, my daughter, Prachi, my very select friends, Aruno Rajratnam, Mr. Kalani, Chandrasekhar, Arun Agarwal, Kaushal Mishra, Rajesh Shah, Alka Sakaria, Bhavang, my cousins, Parul, Rita, Nanda, Kalpana, Dhwani (she has collected all my poems since I started) Meera, Jasmine, Sarla, Preeti, Urmila, Hemal, Prerana all of whom have been my earliest and most appreciative of my readers in my private circulation, my family, Pallavi Vaid, Binal Vaid, Nehal Vaid, my ever supportive father, Mr. Vikram Kotak, and my husband Nainesh, who encourages me in all my endeavours.

Thanks are also owed to Notion Press and my wonderful publishing consultants Mydhili and Isha, and the entire Notion Press team, including my editor, for taking the time and effort to give this book its current shape and form. Any mistakes and lapses are entirely mine and I look forward to hearing from readers their feedback on mail at Uttaravaid.1965@gmail.com.

Dedication

This book is dedicated to the women in my life: my mother, Sita Kotak, my sisters, Sangeeta Chandan and Soni Srivastava, and my daughter, Prachi Vaid, who have always believed me to be smarter than I am and thus made me so…

Contents

On Shiv and Parvati

The First Love Story

Part I: Sati's Self Immolation

Prologue

The first love story between Shiv and Parvati is as dramatic as it can get and spans two lifetimes.

It all began when Brahma wanted Adi Shakti – Shiv's (Adinath's female manifestation) to help him with the creation of the universe, and Shiv, putting the interest of the world at large before His as always, gave her away and renounced the joys of conjugal bliss and became an ascetic.

On completion of the creation of the World, Brahma wanted to return Adi Shakti to Shiv, but alas, she had to be born as a human being and then, attain divinity. Brahma's son Daksh through rigorous penance had asked for Adi Shakti to be reincarnated as his daughter and was granted the boon. Thus was Sati born to him and Prasuti and was the apple of his eye, his favourite among all his daughters.

Brahma then appointed Daksh as the Prajapati to set codes of conduct for the entire humanity, and in order to do this humongous task, he was given inordinate powers to curb indiscipline and ensure that law and order were implemented in human society. Daksh's word was the law and he soon became arrogant enough to believe that he was equivalent to the Tridevs.

Daksh hated Shiv from the bottom of his heart because Shiv was a non-conformist who did not care for the codes, rules, and regulations set in place by Daksh – Shiv was the ultimate free spirit, the Yogi, the strongest and the wisest, the most erudite and knowledgeable, of all spiritual texts, the master of weapons, and all forms of arts from dance to sculpture. But He stayed in Kailash and meditated, and could only be summoned by His staunchest devotees when they were in trouble or when they wanted boons.

Sati was Adi Shakti and was drawn to Shiv who became her all consuming passion. When Daksh heard this, he was livid and did everything in his power to stop Sati from marrying Shiv. He emotionally blackmailed Sati and held a *Swayamvar* for his daughter, where he obviously had not invited Shiv, but worse, installed his statue as a door keeper. Sati ignored all princes and soon, her wedding garland went around the neck of the doorkeeper's (Shiv's) statue. Shiv then manifested himself and married her.

Daksh's fury knew no bounds, and in order to insult Shiv, he announced the grandest *Yagna* of that day and age and deliberately did not invite Sati and Shiv. Sati was very hurt at this omission and vowed to mend the fences between the two men she loved dearly – her father and her husband. Shiv tried everything in His power to stop her but she was her father's daughter, adamant to the core. But as soon as she stepped in the Yagna hall, her fond hopes of facilitating a truce between her father and her husband were dashed. Daksh kept heaping insults on Shiv and poor Sati was heartbroken; she could not bear for her beloved husband to be humiliated thus in front of the entire universe. In those anguished moments, many truths were revealed to her and she decided to self-immolate herself in the Yagna fire.

Here is where the texts differ; some texts relate that she jumped into the Yagna Fire – that's why the practice of Sati, yet others state that Agni Dev declined to burn her, scared of the wrath of Mahadev (Shiv), who was very fond of His young wife. Sati had learnt enough from her Yogi husband even in their marriage of such short tenure and she channelized her inner fire and burnt herself to ashes.

Thus ended the tragic life of Sati but she is soon reborn as Parvati and the first love story takes another dramatic turn. Enjoy Part I – Sati's self-immolation in Sati's words.

1. Part I: Sati's Self Immolation

When I am with Shiv, our hearts beat as one,
I am the luckiest woman, to love so and be loved in return!
And as each miraculous day unfolds, I am awed by his supremacy,
O Lord, how do I overcome my human failings and inadequacy?

Now I hear that my father, steeped in his bitterness and rage,
Has excluded us from his Yagna, refusing still to accept our marriage,
Though uninvited I must go, and make him realise the error of his ways,
Do not worry, Lord, he will welcome his favourite daughter as always!

At the Yagna:
Lord, you coaxed and cajoled and forbade me, and I would not listen,
Now, I have been the cause of your unforgivable humiliation!
This contemptuous man who heaps insults on you, as my father I disown,
Alas as his daughter, I have inherited many of his faults; how do I atone?

This Dakshayani's body and psyche is not worthy of my Lord, it must burn,
But to complete our reunion, in a purer form, I promise you, I will return!

The First Love Story
Part II: Parvati's Resolve

Prologue

Sati (Adishakti's human avatar) had been reborn to Menavati and Himavat, the king of the Himalayas as Parvati. From her childhood spent in Rishi Dadhichi's ashram, Parvati had known that her ultimate destination in life lay in being Shiv's wife.

Like Sati, her every waking moment was spent in loving and dreaming about Shiv and she was assured by all the Rishis of her time, including Markandeya, Dadhichi, and even Devrishi Narad that the entire universe was waiting with eager anticipation for Shiv and Parvati's union. She had been blessed with unparalleled beauty, a virtuous nature, and in keeping with all human criteria was an ideal wife for the Lord Himself, all she had to do was present herself to Him.

Blessed by her parents and all Gods, she enters Shiv's cave to find Him in deep meditation and her courage fails her in declaring her love to Shiv! Indra assures her that he will summon Kaamdev the God of Love to direct arrows filled with love and passion at Shiv, who will then be awakened from His deep meditation and on seeing the beautiful Parvati, will abandon all thoughts of further penance and plunge into matrimony.

So, she was totally unprepared when Shiv, enraged at being disturbed during His meditation, opens His third eye and envelops Kaamdev with flames of His fury and burns him down. Still shaking with anger, He turns down Parvati as well, not paying heed to her ardent pleas and walks out of the cave, livid and furious. Brought up as a beloved daughter of genteel parents, Parvati had never known anger and she was dismayed and heartbroken at thus being rejected. Devastated, she follows Shiv out of the cave and runs into Nandi, Shiv's most ardent devotee, who assures her, harsh though He seemed, Shiv had infinite love for Sati and thus, also for Parvati.

Deeply insulted but reassured, Parvati then resolves that no matter what it takes, she will attain Shiv. Narad also advises her that Shiv may have turned His back on love but no God ever turns His back on *Bhakti* – devotion! This sonnet captures the reassurances given by Nandi who had been witness to the anguish undergone by Shiv in the aftermath of Sati's self-immolation, and Parvati's firm resolve to attain Shiv as His spiritual equal and not just His lady love.

2. Part II: Parvati's Resolve

Nandi to Parvati:

Ever since you have gone, Shiv's love and grief have known no bounds,

He has abandoned Kailash and roamed like a vagabond on earthly grounds,

He has turned into granite with His pent-up fury, anguish, and unshed tears;

Everything that once gave Him happiness has been forsaken for years.

*Shiv, unused to mortal death, in your absence has become a **Shav**[2],*

His smile, His music, His dance will only return with your love!

Parvati to herself:

How foolish I was to assume that Mahadev will fall for my beauty physical,

He is no mere mortal, He will accept me only if I am His spiritual equal!

This time around, I will not hurt my Lord; I will leave nothing to chance,

I will overcome all my human faults by undertaking rigorous penance!

Mahadev, you have seen Sati's obstinacy but not Parvati's determination,

You can reject my love but not my unflinching devotion!

As Sati, I have been the cause of my Lord's unbearable pain,

As Parvati, I will not rest until I bring Him eternal happiness again!

---

2   Shav – A corpse

The First Love Story
Part III: Shiv's Acceptance

Prologue

The third part of the Trilogy delves into Shiv's psyche – at first His rejection of Parvati and then, His acceptance of her. Shiv had, according to himself, married Sati in haste, bowing to the wishes of Lord Vishnu and Brahma and, of course, surrendering to His innate love for Adishakti whose reincarnation was Sati. He had known that Sati was a flawed human being but He had hoped that in time, He would be her guide and Sati's love for Him would mould her into achieving Adishakti's divinity.

Unfortunately, Daksh had been an unforgiving father, whose sole aim in life had been to belittle Shiv at every occasion. In his Yagna, which Shiv had forbidden Sati to attend, Daksh had heaped so many insults on Shiv that Sati could not take it anymore and undertook self-immolation. Her mortal death had plunged Shiv into unbearable grief; He could not forgive himself for not averting this tragedy even though He was omniscient. He had abandoned Kailash, had come close to losing Himself and indeed His divinity, as He carried Sati's corpse in His arms and roamed throughout universe until Vishnu used His Sudarshan to cut it into many pieces. This jolted Shiv out of His self-imposed oblivion and He renounced the world but not before tracing each of her 51 body parts and establishing Shakti *Peeths* at every place where her body part had fallen in fond memory of His young wife.

He had known then, that Adishakti would be born again and would seek Him out as Parvati, indeed when Parvati presented herself to Him, every instinct of His rebelled against accepting her. Like a kaleidoscope, the events of the past flashed before His eyes and He dismissed her when she presented herself to Him, asking her to forget Him instead. But Parvati surprised Him when she undertook the most rigorous penance to please Him not as a lover or a wife but as a devotee. He resolved to himself that at every step, He would create hurdles for her, so she would always fail to reach her destination. So, He did, every time she created a *Shivling* to worship him, the Shivling would be blown to smithereens. He disguised Himself as a Rishi and ridiculed her attempts and tried to dissuade her. He did everything in his power to ensure that her penance did not succeed.

At this point in time, Narad intervenes and remonstrates with Shiv – he asks Shiv to subject Parvati to tests, not as a judge who examines the guilty hoping for their failure to withstand stringent cross examination but as a teacher who also subjects his students to examinations but prays for their success. Shiv then realizes the error of His ways and becomes Parvati's mentor, and when the Lord Himself is a teacher, no student can fail to pass all examinations with flying colours! At the end of her penance, when Shiv goes to meet Parvati, He is taken aback by the complete transformation in her. Gone were her human traits and faults. The woman standing in front of Him had become a Goddess! All His love for Adishakti comes back to Him. There was no hesitation in Him anymore. When He saw the divine manifestation of Adishakti in Parvati, indeed this was the reunion He had been waiting for, for so many aeons. He then accepts Parvati as His wife and with this reunion, the first love story ever recorded in history is concluded and they lived happily ever after...

3. Part III: Shiv's Acceptance

Shiv – when he first saw Parvati

I had loved you, Sati, with all your ego, insecurities, anger, and obstinacy,

Yet, you chose self-immolation to rid yourself of your father's hate legacy.

Parvati, you may be Sati incarnate, marrying you is still a mistake,

I am once bitten, I cannot accept you, even if ordained by fate!

Unfulfilled love had once plunged me into a bottomless abyss,

I am an ascetic now, not for me ever again short-lived conjugal bliss.

Shiv to himself on seeing Parvati's penance

This Parvati is a different person, who has passed all my tests with brilliance,

Her soul has transcended all human barriers and shines with divine luminescence.

Through her intense devotion and penance, she has conquered all five elements;

She is no more a mere mortal but my Adishakti with all her divine embodiments;

She will be a befitting Kali to my Veerbhadra, a true Uma to my Shankar,

After an interminable wait, I must accept her again and become Ardhanarishwar!

Thus the path of true love is never smooth, strewn with obstacles limitless,

It takes even Gods in love several lifetimes to achieve infinite oneness!

Vinayak's Slaying – From Vinayak to Ganesh

Prologue

Vinayak (the name given by Parvati to her child) or Ganpati/ Ganesh's saga is well known to most people. They have probably heard it from their parents/grandparents when they were younger, or the first time they asked, "Why does Ganesh have an elephant head?" but the boon or the curse that led to it are relatively unknown. What is also unknown is that initially, when Shiv met Vinayak, Vinayak had paid obeisance to his father and had very politely refused him entry to his mother's chamber. Shiv had walked away, realizing that whilst children were adamant by nature, it did not behove a great Yogi like him to stoop to the child's level by being unyielding in His demand. However, the eventual beheading of Vinayak by Shiv was also preordained. In fact, a culmination of the manifestation of a boon and a curse.

The curse

Surya, the son of Sage Kashyap, had slowly become quite arrogant on account of his prowess and had once sought to disturb the Yagna of Shiv's two staunch devotees, Mali and Sumali (Who was also the father of Kaikesi, Ravan's mother!) who had a special boon from Shiv that no harm could come to them during Yagna times. When Surya sought to kill these two whilst they were engaged in the worship of Shiv, Shiv had to intervene and kill the arrogant Surya who would not listen to reason. Kashyap Muni was so enraged that he cursed Shiv that one day he would have to use his trident against his own son and only then would he know the pain of a bereaved father! Shiv does bring a chastised Surya to life again and Surya promises that he will never repeat his misdemeanour and use his prowess only for the good of mankind, but the curse had been uttered and could not be foiled.

The boon

Gajasur was a demon who was an ardent devotee of Shiv and he performed severe austerities and penance to appease Shiv. Finally, Ashutosh (another name of Shiv, meaning one who is easily pleased) appears before him and asks him to seek a boon. Since Gajasura always wanted to be known as the most knowledgeable of all living beings and since he knew that only Shiv was the most knowledgeable of all, if only Shiv resided in his psyche, that would be possible. So, he asks for Shiv to reside within him and the Bholenath (Shiv's name, meaning guileless) that Shiv was, immediately grants him this boon and instantly panic sweeps across the three worlds! Vishnu, Brahma, and Parvati are devastated and they hatch a plan and rope in the music maestro Devarshi Narad to assist them. Narad then plays the most divine music in Gajasur's presence, and Gajasur, immensely pleased with Narad, asks him to seek a boon at which all three, Narad, Brahma, and Vishnu, manifest themselves before Gajasur and ask him to release Shiv from his psyche. Gajasur agrees on the condition that he should constantly remain in the presence of Shiv and his elephant head should be known as the most knowledgeable of all living beings. The trio immediately agrees to these conditions and informs Gajasur that soon, things will be so ordained that Nandi will come seeking Gajasur's head which he should give up of his own free will. This will eventually be attached to the body of Shiv's slayed son thus meeting both Gajasur's conditions.

Thus, the entire slaying was pre-ordained, indeed Shiv, omniscient as He was, knew what was to follow, even though He refuses to rise to the bait until Vinayak attacks Him first! To which, I have added some poetic licence to make it relevant for our modern times...

4. Vinayak's Slaying - From Vinayak to Ganesh

Parvati

Swami, is this why I waited years for your homecoming,

To suffer your fury and witness my beloved Vinayak's slaying?

From this anguish shall emerge untold destruction and unending pain,

Until you redeem this colossal mistake and resurrect our son again!

Shiv

Parvati, remember you poured life into a mound of your post bath unguents,

The final product always carries the characteristics of its ingredients!

His arrogant and impure mind would not listen to reason or bow to sentiment,

He has added insult to injury against my devotees and flung weapons at his parent!

You are not just the mother of this child but of the entire universe,

If an errant child is not disciplined young, he grows up to be much worse,

I see no option but to substitute this head which houses his terrible brain,

With an enlightened, righteous psyche, thus shall our Ganesh be born again.

And thus was set the age old tradition of the father being the disciplinarian,

Because like Parvati, a mother still cannot see the faults of her children!

Vrinda's Curse

Prologue

This poem of mine links one incident of Vishnu's life to all His human avatars! If you have ever wondered, why Ram, Krishna, or even Gautam Buddha never enjoyed a good love life, you need to go back in history to Vrinda.

Vishnu had Vrinda's curse on him. Vrinda was the chaste and pious wife of Jalandhar who was Shivaansh, i.e., a part of Shiv, who is also recognized by many scriptures as Shiv's son! He had been nurtured by Shukracharya, the Asura Guru, to have complete dominion over all three worlds – a *Trilokadhipati!* He hated the Devas and swore to destroy them.

In those days, it was believed that a pious wife's (A Sati's) chastity gave an invincible armour to her husband's valour in war. Vrinda was such a Sati and her husband was close to achieving invincibility and immortality. Vishnu had to foil this before it happened, and he could see no other option but to destroy Vrinda's chastity! This was a very difficult decision because Vrinda was a devout Vishnu devotee and a God protects His devotees instead of violating them! However, Vishnu goes ahead with His decision, and in Jalandhar's absence, disguises Himself as Jalandhar and takes His place in Vrinda's life.

In retrospect, this seems almost unbelievable and you would think that if Vishnu indeed was God, surely, He could have used other means and devices at His disposal to achieve Jalandhar's end, but that was not to be. When Vrinda finds out the truth, she is shattered! To think that she had been deceived by the deity she had worshipped all her life, the God for whom she had argued endlessly with the man she loved and married and who had loved her in return! And to further realise that her chastity was stained for ever…

This poem captures her anguish, when she is at the brink of ending her life, her fury at being deceived, and her curse and also Vishnu's remorse and his singular thought process that defined all His future avatars also.

The only way, I could destroy Mahadev's son,
Was by destroying you;
Every time virtue sides with evil,
It shall be destroyed too!

5. Vrinda's Curse

Vrinda

Oh, Vishnu, epitome of virtue, whom I have worshipped all my life,
How could you pretend to be my husband and take me as your wife?
I have lost both my husband and my God; I feel nothing but anguish,
Now, my defiled chastity mocks me, death is my only wish!

Vishnu, I curse you today, you shall be turned to stone and atone,
Your love of life shall forever elude you and you will be helpless alone,
You too shall suffer pangs of separation, your love, you too shall miss,
Lord of the Universe, you shall have everything except conjugal bliss!

Vishnu

I am guilty as charged, Vrinda, but it has torn my heart asunder,
Your unblemished chastity had become Jalandhar's invincible armour.
I accept all your curses, Vrinda, and you will be reborn as Shaligram's Tulsi.
Our illicit union now will forever be sanctified through holy matrimony.

And in all my avatars, I shall be denied love's much splendored glory,
Be it Sita, Radha, or Yashodhara, Vishnu will repent throughout history!

From
The Ramayan

Hẽ Ram – A Devotee's Plea

Prologue to Poems 6 and 7

As mentioned in the foreword, this was my first sonnet, after my discovery, that Uttar Kand of Ramayan never really happened but is an appendage to the original Valmiki Ramayan! As I read more and more about Ram from different sources, the fact that Ram was much ahead of his times emerged. Ram is not a king or an individual. The word 'Ram' encompasses an entire lifetime of ideal conduct in all circumstances and in all relationships! This is a lifetime which serves as a beacon to mankind generations later, on what is right and righteous, a conduct to be emulated by mankind centuries later when circumstances may have changed, but human dilemmas remain much the same.

Therefore this note serves as a prologue to both poems numbered 6 and 7; Hẽ Ram and Ram Against Blind Tradition. They are both composed to serve as a personal catharsis for me – oh how could I even believe my God to be guilty of reprehensible conduct, why wasn't my faith in Him strong, why hadn't I trusted Him more? There will be oblique references to other sonnets also from this collection where context demands it, so that a clear picture of Ram emerges as an iconoclast, much ahead of his times – a man who balanced both the Qa and the Qi in his nature so beautifully.

In his every relationship, he brought to it a certain gravitas, dignity, sensitivity, and a tenderness which only complemented his strength as a warrior and an amazing strategist. Not for him was alpha machoism at the altar of empathy or righteousness! If, through aeons and centuries, one man's conduct could be or should be emulated by posterity, there is no better example than Ram throughout history!

As a **son**, much has been said, how on the eve of coronation, he gives up Ayodhya's throne and proceeds towards the forest. No trace of either martyrdom or anger, whether at his father, Dashrath, or his stepmother, Kaikeyi, a son tasked with the sole purpose of fulfilling his father's vows so that his or his dynasty's reputation does not get besmirched! Also refer to Poem No. 8; Shanta's Sacrifice, where he observes his mother's melancholy and gets her to confide her angst to him and makes amends for things buried in the past and long forgotten. And to the sonnet 9, Ram's letter to Kaikeyi, where he realizes that in obeying his Guru's orders, he may have inadvertently hurt Kaikeyi's feelings immeasurably.

As a **prince**, how he follows Vishwamitra into the forests, no questions asked, when Vishwamitra asks Dashrath to lend his sons to him so that the region could be cleared of vicious demons who did not allow any Yagna to be performed peacefully! After Dashrath's Ashwamedha Yagna, when the white stallion had to be sacrificed, how Ram intervened and got the officiating priests to agree to finish the ceremony by sacrificing a golden replica of the horse instead of killing it! How he insisted on going into Ahalya's hut without being prejudiced by public opinion that doing so would invite the wrath of the sages on him and his dynasty.

As a **husband**, how he promises monogamy in letter and spirit to Sita There were very few kings in those times who took vows like that, they were, in fact, encouraged to be polygamous if political necessity demanded the same!, how he gives in to her wish to accompany him to the forest (he had famously declared then, "I wouldn't go to heaven without you, Sita!") and how he is always respectful, loving, caring, and protective of her throughout their exile, until she is abducted by Ravan! And then, the resolute determination of a husband truly in love, who vows to get her back, never suspecting her fidelity (refer to Sonnet no. 16 Sita's Trial by Fire), a man who had only his bow and arrow and his brother on this quest, his wife kidnapped by a Trilokadhipati -- the rulers of all three realms, Swarga Lok, Prithvi Lok, and Pataal Lok, almost a mission impossible!

As a **brother**, whilst Ram's constant companion has always been Lakshman, history has recorded his genuine fondness for Bharat. This was evident when Kaikeyi sought his forgiveness and he smiled and confessed; he could never have any ill feeling for a mother who had given him a brother like Bharat! His love for Lakshman comes to the fore in the only instance he loses his equanimity during the war. This is when Lakshman lies on the battlefield grievously wounded by Meghnad, and Ram sees Lakshman's life ebbing away, and he sobs uncontrollably on the battlefield!

As an **enemy** – even as an enemy, Ram stands unparalleled in history, he sends peace emissaries twice with the objective of avoiding war at all costs, but when war was inevitable, he becomes a true leader and commander and transforms his unlikely army of apes into an indomitable unit. Every time a warrior from the enemy camp fell to his arrows, in the evening, the dead body was sent respectfully with every body part reattached, to the enemy camp so that the last rites of the warrior could be performed as per scriptures!

Ram truly was an ideal man. Therefore, when thought logically, without doubt, all the main three episodes, in Uttar Kand seem fictitious and completely contrived to further the vested interests of India's conquerors through the ages, who had sought mass scale conversions from Hinduism to other religions and to play in the hands of the powerful Brahmins who wanted to re-establish their dominance in the society of those times. Consider these three defining episodes of Uttar Kand!

- There is absolutely no way that Ram would have abandoned Sita when she needed him most; during her pregnancy, to the forest, in fact, Lakshman also would have remonstrated with his brother, just as he did when Ram had demanded that Sita walk through fire before being reunited with him, after his victory over Ravan! (Refer to Sonnet No. 16; Sita's Trial By Fire)

- There is no way that Ram would have allowed Lakshman to take Jal Samadhi, forget his sentencing Lakshman to death, over Lakshman's failure to fulfil his instruction of being undisturbed. This was supposedly when he was having a private meeting with Kaal and Sage Durvasa demanded an instant audience with Ram!

- Even more unbelievable, is Ram ordering that Shambuk, a Shudra be beheaded for the "crime" of mastering the Vedas, thus granting exclusive rights over all spiritual literature of the times to the Brahminical society!

Since all of the above are not by any stretch of imagination, even remotely reflective of Ram or what he stood for, what he embodied, the only natural conclusion is that this never happened – this is where mythology (the word 'mythology' owes its origin to the word myth, that which is untrue!) takes over history!

And therein lies his divinity, despite such obvious scurrilous attempts at vilification, only God could continue to be worshipped throughout the ages with such devotion! And therein lies my naivete also. Ram does not need to explain or defend himself...

6. Hẽ Ram – A Devotee's Plea!

Ram, banished from your kingdom on the eve of your coronation,
You bore no malice towards Mother Kaikeyi, no indignation!
Ram, you were the first to take a stand against sexual discrimination,
If Indra remains unpunished, why should Ahilya be denied salvation?

And on your wedding night, you gifted Sita the ultimate pledge of monogamy,
A Raghuvanshi's promise, there shall be no other woman but you for me!
For whom, you moved heaven and earth to get her back,
You could have never abandoned her, how can anybody believe that?

Ram, you who accorded the highest respect to all women,
Come just once to earth again and tell the disbelieving heathen,
Tell them that you never banished Sita, her exile never happened,
The Uttar Kand, an appendage is your carefully orchestrated vilification!

Hẽ Ram, a devotee pleads, for once break your constraint and piety,
Hẽ Ram, come and save yourself from your own notoriety!

7. Ram Against Blind Tradition

They said

Ram, sacrificing the Ashwamedh stallion is a foregone conclusion,
Tradition demands a living being's sacrifice not a metallic impersonation!

Ram

No life that has served my country shall be sacrificed at my stake,
Beheading him, instead of rewarding him would be a colossal mistake!

They said

Ram, do not venture that way, there lies Ahilya's hermitage,
Tradition dictates, if you free her, you shall suffer the rage of a sage.

Ram

Blind superstition cannot stop me, If I can, I must help her,
Ahilya has been a victim, of treachery, and her husband's anger.

Ram

The most evolved of all species, how can mankind follow traditions blind?
To discern between right and wrong is the duty of every human mind!
That which harbours cruelty or violence is neither religion nor tradition,
But reflects the vested interests of depraved elements, their mental subversion!

That country can never prosper, which does not question religion or tradition,
And then, accepts only those which satisfy the ethics and morality of every citizen!

Shanta's Sacrifice – Her Untold Story

Prologue

Most people who have read the Ramayan know that Dashrath – the King of Ayodhya – had been advised to get the Putra Kameshthi Yagna (A Yagna performed for the sole purpose of begetting progeny) performed by Rishi Rishyasringa, who was famous for his innate chastity because he had been brought up by his father and had never set eyes on a woman during his formative years. However, Rishi Rishyasringa had to perform this Yagna after getting married to an equally chaste woman for the Yagna to be successful and produce the desired result.

As we all know, the Yagna was performed successfully and yielded two portions of the sacred offering, which the Sage gave to Dashrath's eldest queen, Kaushalya, and his middle queen, Kaikeyi. Kaushalya and Kaikeyi shared half of their offering with Sumitra, the youngest queen, so that she could be a mother as well. In due course, Kaushalya gave birth to Ram, and her half of the offering that she had given to Sumitra, took birth as Lakshman. Kaikeyi gave birth to Bharat and her half of the offering was born as Shatrughan to Sumitra, who had given birth to twins. This explains the inseparable bonds that existed between Ram and Lakshman and between Bharat and Shatrughan.

Soon, the four princes completed their education and returned from Guru Vashistha's Ashram to a rousing welcome in Ayodhya. But Ram's observant eyes detected a pall of gloom which seemed to envelop Kaushalya. Even when her lips were smiling, pain lurked in her eyes and the sensitive Ram could not bear to see his mother so unhappy and not know the reason why. So, one day, when a private conducive moment presented itself, he very gently asked his mother the reason behind her misery.

Queen Kaushalya, tired of bearing the grief all by herself, broke down when she heard the kindness in Ram's voice and this poem captures the conversation between Kaushalya and Ram as she unburdens her secrets to Ram – the secret of Shanta – her and Dashrath's first born – and the mystery behind Rishi Rishyasringa's marriage, the sage who performed the Putra Kameshthi Yagna and the hidden facts surrounding the birth of Ram and his brothers.

8. Shanta's Sacrifice – Her Untold Story

Kaushalya to Ram

My first-born Shanta was beautiful, wise and in the battlefield, second to none,
But none of her accomplishments mattered to her father, he wanted a son!
Would the glorious Ishkvaku dynasty die with him, he worried to his bone,
He could not die in peace, without giving a future king to Ayodhya's throne!

If only Rishyasringa and his wife could perform the Yagna to beget us a son,
But getting the chaste Rishyasringa to marry was easier said than done!
Your father sent many pretty maidens and his worry grew with every failure,
And then, Shanta resolved, she would return only after succeeding in her endeavour!

She went, she saw, and conquered the heart of Rishyasringa who gladly married her,
The yagna was performed and the birth of four princes assured Ayodhya's future!
She lives in an austere hut now atop a hill and with guilt my heart is torn,
She who could have been a queen, gave up everything so you could be born!

And it follows
Even centuries later, a daughter will make every sacrifice, bear every pain,
Just so that she can bring a smile on her unhappy father's face again!

Ram's Letter to Kaikeyi

Prologue

The title of this poem may already have piqued your curiosity; when did Ram ever write a letter to Kaikeyi? But again, to appreciate the circumstances and the content thereof, it would be necessary to delve a little into the past.

Among the four brothers, it was a well-known fact that Kaikeyi doted on Ram; Ram was her undoubted favourite. Perhaps, Kaikeyi was a perfectionist and Ram had all the attributes that she was looking for, he was superlative in everything he was taught, from scriptures to warfare and combined in himself a rare sensitivity, consideration, and wisdom. Though her natural born was Bharat, he never measured up to her high standards, and was so much inclined towards poetry, painting, and fine arts that she sent him away to Kaikeya to train under her brother and father in all princely pursuits. And like all mothers, she had forever dreamt of choosing Ram's bride and presiding over the most spectacular wedding for the prince of Kosala. (Kosala was the country and Ayodhya was the capital).

Alas, this was not to be, because as we know history, Ram won Sita's hand in her *Swayamvar* by breaking *Shivdhanush* (Shiv's bow). As custom had it, the wedding would still have to be solemnized by seeking the consent of the groom's parents and inviting them to the wedding. Janak had sent out the invite but when there was an inordinate delay in receiving a response from Ayodhya, Ram, who had been camping with Guru Vishwamitra in Rishi Yagnavalkya's ashram outside Mithila, sensed that this delay must be on account of Kaikeyi being miffed. Kaikeyi had reasons though, Mithila could not hold a candle to the territory, power, and riches of Kosala, besides Kaikeyi was also made aware (by who else but Manthara!), that Sita was not Janak's natural born, but she was found in a farm when in order to end a 12-year famine in his kingdom, Janak was advised to plough the field himself.

Ram then sends out this letter to Kaikeyi, on reading which, she immediately gives her consent (Now, your curiosity should be more piqued, just what was in the letter that mollified and pacified Kaikeyi instantly?) and more so, she also gives this letter that she treasured as her most precious welcome gift to Sita.

If the purpose of Ram's avatar was to live a life that men could emulate for centuries, there is no better example than this communication with his mother- which youngsters in love today can learn from, to placate their miffed mothers in agreeing to their choice. It starts by very delicately hinting at the fact that Ram knew that Sita was not Kaikeyi's choice, a subtle apology for having deprived Kaikeyi of her dream. What follows, however, is the stroke of a genius. Ram says that in every way, Sita reminded him of Kaikeyi and then, after eulogizing all of Kaikeyi's qualities, he tugs at her heart strings and very cleverly rests the decision making on her. If there is one forever correct answer to the perennial question of "what women want", it is this – let them decide. If you are confident of their love for you, if the final decision determining your happiness is left to them, they will always decide in your favour. He also very cleverly refrains from declaring his love for Sita, sensing that women cannot accept competition easily in matters of the heart.

9. Ram's Letter to Kaikeyi

Kaikeyi – visibly angry

A marriage must be among equals, compared to Kosala, Mithila is a but a village;
Ayodhya's future queen must hail from royal lineage, not be the daughter of a sage!

Besides, how can I accept an orphan picked up from the rural countryside,
When I can have the most beautiful accomplished princess to be my Ram's bride?

Ram - in his letter to Kaikeyi

Sita, though not your choice, has your persona, your grace, and your fine nature;
Her every regal stance, every compassionate glance, reminds me of you, O Mother!

Just as in Kaikeya and Ayodhya, it is you; who rules over everybody heart;
She is Mithila's daughter, just like you; no ordinary mortal, but a class apart!

Unexpected circumstances have conspired to bring us together in this relation,
But this union cannot come to fruition, without your blessings and permission!

Kaikeyi – on reading the letter

Her eyes glistening with unshed tears, her voice quivering with emotion,
She declared, I shall not fail you, Ram, if your happiness depends on my decision!

So, centuries later, to date,
Overcoming all personal objections, a mother eventually gives in to her child's happiness,
Because to every mother, her child is both, her unfailing strength and her biggest weakness!

A Debate of Sacrifice

Prologue

This particular conversation between Ram and Bharat holds tremendous significance in many different aspects of our rich ancient history because it shines a spotlight on sacrifice, on brotherly love, on strict moral codes by which our ancient kings lived and died, and on the democratic governance norms of the ancient monarchies.

This debate happens soon after Bharat Milap – in the gut-wrenching emotionally charged atmosphere, when Bharat with the queen mothers, Guru Vashishtha and his ministers, army and his subjects, goes to Chitrakoot, with only one unshakeable objective – to convince Ram to take back what was rightfully his, the kingship of the mighty and prosperous Kosala with Ayodhya as its capital. So determined was Bharat to set right the injustice done by Maharani Kaikeyi that he had gone with the full regalia necessary for the coronation of Ram in the forest itself as the rightful monarch of Kosala and to bring him back to Ayodhya so that the country got the king they had always wanted!

However, Ram was equally resolute and determined. Under no circumstances would he go back or reclaim the kingdom that had been promised to Bharat by his father. He would neither sully the memory of his dead father, nor dishonour the vows given by a descendant of the Raghuvanshi dynasty.

The arguments on both sides were equally forceful and convincing; eventually, it was decided that this serious debate needed a pious, righteous arbitrator whose decision would be respected and considered binding by both parties. Guru Vashishtha recused himself from this onerous task as being too close to the family, and it fell on Rajrishi Janak, the father-in-law of both brothers – the sage king of Mithila – to arbitrate on this important issue.

Herein also lies the political significance of this debate. The fact that this would decide the ultimate ruler of Kosala was not left to the family but was decided through a presiding judge in front of the citizenry whose future this decision would ultimately affect.

Bharat uses every reasoning. He declares his refusal to ever ascend the throne that was thrust upon him by the evil designs of Queen Kaikeyi. He reminds Ram of his kingly duties (*Rajdharm*); he knew Ram held Rajdharm paramount in his strict moral code. He beseeches Ram to restore the happiness of his subjects and his family and finally, reminds Ram of the love they shared as brothers.

But Ram does not relent! Not even when Queen Kaikeyi apologises to her subjects, to Ram, and takes back her boons so that Ram is released from his obligation towards their fulfilment!

This debate is also significant in Rajrishi Janak's judgement, while he holds love, worship, and devotion paramount (Though a whole *Yug* later, Krishna also propounds *Bhakti Yog* superior to *Jnana* and *Karma Yog* though each is but a different way of leading the devotee to God), he shows Bharat the true meaning of selfless love. And therein lies the true irony of this debate; there is no loser because this is a debate of sacrifice, not of personal gain, nor for victory, but for setting the foundation of a righteous and moral code that respects both love and duty.

Because Bharat wins, Ram had to accept the kingship of Kaushal on his return. How does Ram win? He gets Bharat to accept his decision of first fulfilling his vow to his father of fourteen years' exile before his coronation!

10. A Debate of Sacrifice

Bharat

Brother, it is always the eldest who is the rightful heir to the Ishkvaku throne,

Your kingly duties command you to return to your subjects now miserable and forlorn!

Shame be on me, if I succumb to such evil design and commit such unpardonable sin,

If the vows demand, throne to one son and exile to the other,

I will take the forest, you be the king!

Ram

Our father sacrificed everything, to uphold his promises and preserve their sanctity,

Reneging on the same after his death, will be an indelible blot forever on our dynasty!

Mother Kaikeyi can take back her words, but I do not have that option,

As sons and Raghuvanshis, fulfilling those vows is our only redemption!

Bharat

Brother, if you do not return, I shall fast unto death and quit living,

Ram

Bharat, dying is easier for me than a lifetime of regret and sin!

Janak

Bharat succeeds in this debate, because even Gods bow to love and devotion,

But Bharat, true and selfless love demands acquiescence to the loved one's decision!

And thus ends the debate of sacrifice, in which both love and duty win,

Ram accepts the throne after fourteen years of Bharat's representative reign!

Sita's Sisters – The Unsung Heroines

Prologue

This poem is based on the three sisters of Sita - Mandvi, Urmila, and Shrutkirti – who also faced the storm in their lives and the unforeseen changes brought about by Ram's exile accompanied by Sita and Laxman. There is so little known about their sacrifices that they are relegated to history as inconsequential to the main narrative - and in their story lies the story of every woman, who does so much for her family but her efforts remain unseen and unappreciated.

Mandvi, Bharat's wife

Bharat was so distraught when he heard of his beloved brother's exile for fourteen years and when all his attempts at bringing Ram back failed, he left the palace, set up his own hermitage outside the city, and for fourteen years, lived the life of a celibate *sanyasi*. In doing so, he wanted to punish his mother, Kaikeyi, whom he could not bear to see for the injustice she had done. So, while history has recorded Laxman's separation from his wife Urmila, for fourteen years, Mandvi's sacrifice and loneliness for those fourteen years has largely gone unnoticed.

Urmila, Laxman's wife

Urmila knew that for Laxman, his brother, Ram, came before every other relationship Laxman had, and it would be futile to hold him back from accompanying Ram on his exile. Laxman was in a dilemma, for these fourteen years of living in the wild, he had to be vigilant at all times, to protect his brother and *Bhabhi (sister-in-law)* from the dangers lurking in the forest at night. He, therefore, pleads with Nidra Devi – the Goddess of Sleep – to exempt him from sleep. She agrees, provided he finds somebody who agrees to take his share of sleep for those fourteen years and lie in a vegetative state, almost in a coma. Urmila, his wife, smilingly agrees to bear this burden, and as a result, is overcome by slumber for all those fourteen years of Ram's exile.

Shrutkirti, Shatrughan's wife

The youngest of the sisters, who had protested that she was actually too young to get married, was assured by Sita that she would take care of Shrutkirti because all four sisters were married in the same household. She was a very young bride, totally unprepared for matrimony, but her heart went out to her husband who being the youngest of the brothers, had to handle the massive responsibility of a caretaker king. Every night, Shatrughan came to her, worried at his every inexperienced decision and confided in her that he was terrified and he might make a mistake that would forever stain the unblemished reputation of Raghukul dynasty. In the absence of elders, the young couple had to grow up fast and sacrifice their joys in the process.

This poem recounts their turmoil, their anxieties, and the innumerable sacrifices and compromises made by these three sisters, so that happy times could return to Ayodhya again!

11. Sita's Sisters – The Unsung Heroines

Mandvi to Bharat

You have abandoned me, the palace, gone to live a celibate sanyasi's life,

Between, overpowering guilt and brotherly love, have you thought of your wife?

How is it that a woman can never renounce her duties and walk away too?

You may have wanted to punish your mother, but I am punished too!

Urmila to Laxman

I shall not hold you back, I shall smilingly accept my fate.

Because I know, Ram resides in every breath you take!

All your duties are mine too, in times so unfortunate,

Fourteen years, you shall be exempt from sleep, while I lie inanimate!

Shrutkirti to herself

Nothing causes more anxiety than premature responsibility suddenly thrust,

When all dust settles down, those who are left behind must,

Keep a brave face, sacrifice their joys, and take care of everything,

True, uneasy lies the head that wears the crown even of a caretaker king!

And thus, women have always bravely and calmly overcome every disaster,

Her battles may remain unseen, but every woman is an unsung warrior!

Bali Vadh – The Slaying of Bali

Prologue

One of the most dramatic conversations in ancient history is the dialogue between Bali and Ram, after Ram walks over to Bali who has been grievously wounded by Ram's arrow shot from behind a bush when Bali had been engaged and had overpowered his bother Sugreev in a duel.

Bali, the king of Kishkindha, was a mighty warrior and was known to possess the strength of 70,000 elephants (Bhim was said to possess the strength of 10,000 elephants) and you can gauge his strength from that yardstick!

Bali had a boon from Brahma in the form of a necklace with golden beads, which he always wore around his neck during war times, that half the strength of his opponent would flow into him, thus making him far stronger than his already weakened opponent. Bali was, therefore, invincible in a head-to-head combat. Among his contemporaries, Bali had also defeated Ravan and had traversed the entire earth with Ravan under his armpit for three months, after which Ravan begged for mercy and signed a truce with him.

Bali and Sugreev were loving brothers, until one day challenged by Asur Mayavi (Dundubhi's brother who had been earlier killed by Bali, also Ravan's wife Mandodari's brother) he chases Mayavi into a cave and instructs Sugreev to keep guard at the mouth of the cave until he vanquished Mayavi and emerged. Sugreev waited and then, at the end of a month, saw blood trickling out of the cave. He heard a piercing scream and mistakenly thought that Mayavi had killed Bali, and in order to save himself and his kingdom, he places a huge boulder at the mouth of the cave and proceeds towards Kishkindha.

He is then declared the king of Kishkindha, but alas it was Bali who had defeated Mayavi and was enraged at being trapped in the cave. Mighty as he was, Bali moves the boulder, comes to Kishkindha, and is furious to see Sugreev on the throne. He gives no chance to Sugreev to explain, but brands him a traitor and would have killed him, had Sugreev not taken refuge in Rishimukh mountain, where on account of an earlier curse, Bali was denied entry.

Weeks of solitude in the cave had changed Bali, and in his second reign, he was arrogant, quite vicious, and had also forced himself upon Ruma, Sugreev's wife, disregarding all counsel from Tara, his very beautiful and virtuous wife.

Hanuman then introduced Ram to Sugreev, who was wandering in search of his own wife abducted by Ravan. When Ram heard Sugreev's heart wrenching story, he immediately took it upon himself to redeem this injustice and in return, Sugreev promised him all assistance in uniting him with Sita. Ram then asks Sugreev to challenge Bali to a duel, and hides behind a tree (knowing fully well that in a head-to-head combat, Bali was invincible) and at an opportune moment, fells him with his arrow.

He walks up to him and what follows is a Bali writhing in pain from his fatal wound, demanding to know why Ram did what he did! This conversation forms the crux of the poem below, and it is to Ram's credit and a mark of respect to the mighty warrior Bali once was, that he answers each of Bali's questions until Bali finally recognizes his divinity and begs pardon.

Ram also accepts that his deed too was not completely free of consequences and as karmic justice, in Dwapar Yug,

Bali is reborn as Jara who mistakes a sleeping Krishna for a deer and shoots him with his arrow, thus leading Krishna to the end of his human birth.

12. Bali Vadh (The slaying of Bali)

Bali

You killed me by deceit, you known for courage, wisdom, and strict morality,
I was not even your enemy; how will you ever justify this blot on your dynasty?

Ram

Those who talk of moral righteousness must themselves be above reproach,
In your last moments, think of your sins, the realms of vice that you encroached!
You banished your brother under false suspicion, bloodthirsty and ready to kill,
And more unpardonable was forcing yourself on his wife against her will.

Bali

But our codes are different, and this is not even your kingdom,
So, what right do you have to punish me, for any misdeeds I may have done?

Ram

Have you forgotten, as a king, your actions invite emulation
from your subjects, deriving from your acts a royal sanction?
To uphold right is my right, to destroy wrong is my mission,
And nobody shall be forgiven, if he indulges in rape or abduction.

Because a crime against a woman is a crime against entire humanity,
From which nobody, not even a king, can be granted immunity!

Kumbhakaran

Prologue

For long in our religious texts, Kumbhakaran (meaning pot-ears), Ravan's younger brother has been reduced to a caricature of a giant lost in hedonistic pleasures of only sleeping and eating, and little is known about his finer aspects as an erudite philosopher, a knowledgeable inventor, a loyal brother, and a fierce warrior!

Like his other two brothers, Kumbhakaran was also well versed in the scriptures and vedas, and his brilliance in war was enhanced on account of his massive dimensions (he was 600 bows tall and 100 bows wide) aided by his constant research and development of new and improved weapons in his arsenal. In fact, he was such a keen student that Devrishi Narad had taught him philosophy personally and in one of his (Narad's) unguarded moments, had confided in him that Lord Vishnu in His human avatar would be the nemesis of both Ravan and Kumbhakaran.

Indra, the king of Gods, was terrified of Kumbhakaran, having tasted defeat at his hands in a prior battle. So, when Indra heard that all three brothers were performing severe penance, he was worried that as a boon, Kumbhakaran was sure to ask for Indra's throne! Therefore, when it was time for Lord Brahma to grant Kumbhakaran a boon, Indra pleaded with Saraswati Devi to garble his tongue. In any case, Saraswati and Brahma were very concerned that on account of his humongous appetite, a constantly hungry Kumbhakaran could pose a severe threat to the food reserves of the world.

So, when Lord Brahma manifested himself to Kumbhakaran and asked him to seek a boon, Kumbhakaran who had intended to seek *Indrasana* (Indra's asana – his throne), ended up muttering *Nidrasana* – the state of constant sleep. Brahma quickly said *Tathastu* and would have disappeared, but a quick-thinking Ravan stopped him and pleaded for some relief to his dear brother from a state of perennial slumber! Brahma relented and modified his boon so that Kumbhakaran slept for six months and then got up for a day, enjoyed a royal repast and other pursuits until sleep claimed him again for another six months.

This continued until Sita was abducted, and on Surpanakha's goading, Kumbhakaran, in a fit of rage, went to kill Sita, but he had been such a pious soul until then, that on seeing Sita, he immediately saw Goddess Lakshmi's manifestation in her and his rage abated. He then took it upon himself to reform Ravan and persuade him to do the right thing by returning Sita with full honour and abandoning war by seeking pardon from Ram.

Kumbhakaran – the sonnet captures this conversation and also captures the conversation Kumbhakaran has on the battlefield with Vibhishan just before the war was to begin for the day. Vibhishan knew that Kumbhakaran was a deeply righteous man and would not do anything that his moral values did not permit. He persuaded Kumbhakaran to side with the right and abandon the wrong! Kumbhakaran is not swayed by Vibhishan's contentions – accepting that Ravan had indeed made a mistake, remembering Narad's prophecy, knowing fully well that death and defeat were certain in any war against Lord Vishnu himself – but still choosing to go ahead and fight on Ravan's side.

In both these conversations, Kumbhakaran emerges as a man who did not hesitate to speak his mind and exemplified the philosophy that righteousness is personal and subjective and differs from individual to individual. His last wishes enunciated to both his brothers – to Ravan to save himself and his country, showed how deeply he cared for both and to Vibhishan to perform their last rites as the sole surviving member of the Asur clan showed his religious bent of mind.

13. Kumbhakaran

Kumbhakaran to Ravan

In abducting the Mother Goddess, you have committed an unpardonable sin;

A king who does not heed well-meaning advice subjects his kingdom to ruin.

It is not too late to seek pardon and return Sita to her husband with honour,

But if you must insist on war, I shall fight till my last breath with valour!

However, If I meet martyrdom, know that Narad's prophecy has come true,

Save yourself and Lanka, because you shall not be fighting Ram but Lord Vishnu!

Kumbhakaran to Vibhishan (on the battlefield)

I do not agree with your ethics or morality. Yes, Ravan made a mistake,

But when one's limb gets diseased, the body does not always amputate!

Besides, aren't you committing a worse sin, by betraying your country and family,

Do you think history will ever forgive you for joining hands with the enemy ?

I shall not abandon my country or my family when they need me most,

But as a favour, do perform our last rites well, when our lives are lost!

And through centuries

Kumbhakaran may have lost the war, but is remembered with respect and admiration;

And Vibhishan may have won, but has been tainted with a defector's besmirched reputation!

Ravan – His Last Sermon

Prologue

Ravan remains one of the most fascinating characters of our ancient history and not just of Ramayan. He was so accomplished and so knowledgeable in so many different disciplines that he remains without parallel in the realms of history. The only monarch who used an aeroplane (*Pushpak*) as his personal mode of transport speaks volumes of his engineering acumen, his invention of the Rudra Veena from his limbs as his tribute to Shiv his deity and his mastery over the instrument not only gives evidence of his devotion to Shiv, but also a deep musical talent. His composition of the *Shiv Strotra* shows his literary bent of mind. The fact that Ram requests Ravan to officiate as a Brahmin at his Rameshwaram Puja shows that he had mastered the Vedas and Puranas way beyond any of his contemporaries.

In order to understand Ravan better, it would be necessary to know a little about his previous births, where as guardians of Brahmalok, he (Jay) and his colleague (Vijay), had offended the Sanatkumars who cursed them to lose their official positions in Brahmalok and forever be humans. They prayed to Lord Vishnu to release them from this curse who offered them a choice – they could choose to be His followers and disciples, and after seven lifetimes on Earth, their position would be restored to them, or they could choose to be His mortal enemies and after three lifetimes, they could come back to their official duties. Ravan chose the latter, knowing fully well that if he chose to be the Lord's mortal enemy, he would die at the hands of Lord Himself and this would also shorten the period of his curse to three lifetimes.

So, in the first lifetime, they were born as Harinakshyapu and Harinakshu – who were killed by the Lord Himself in his Narsimha Avatar, in their second lifetimes, they were born as Ravan and Kumbhakaran who were killed by Ram, and in their third avatars, they were born as Kansa and Shishupal who were killed by Krishna.

Is it any wonder that when Ravan was dying, Ram asked Lakshman to request Ravan to impart his last words of wisdom so that humanity benefits from the same? Lakshman goes to Ravan, stands at his head, and "demands" instruction to which Ravan flatly refuses, as a victor, Lakshman was entitled to his land and riches but not to his wisdom! Laksman is then instructed by Ram to stand at his feet and beseech Ravan – who had by then realized that Ram was none other than Lord Vishnu and his death was pre-ordained at Ram's hands.

This sonnet captures those words of wisdom which were shared with Lakshman by Ravan at his deathbed and the fact that they are as relevant today after so many aeons is testimony to the erudition of Ravan and how knowledgeable Ravan truly was!

14. Ravan – His Last Sermon

Ravan to Lakshman

Now that you stand by my feet, not as a victor, but as a seeker,
Lakshman, I accept you as my disciple and shall be your teacher.

As a first, never reveal your intimate secrets to any other man,
If you cannot keep your own secrets, nobody else can!

Never underestimate your enemy, I always held men and monkeys in derision,
Today, they are my nemesis, against whom I never sought divine protection!

Never ill-treat people closest to you, your charioteer, cook, or your brother,
They can be your best friends or worst enemies, like no other!

Never delay good intent, but do not rush where angels fear to tread,
Procrastinate and review, where doubt persists, even the slightest shred!

Even the mightiest monarch must conquer his internal enemies,
I have been destroyed by my ego and covetousness, not your armies!

Thus, as Ravan counted his last breath and awaited death, he smiled with satisfaction,
Just one more lifetime, one more death at His hands, and then, his final destination!

Mandodari – On Ravan's Demise

Prologue

This poem is on Mandodari, Ravan's chief consort and his lady love! Mandodari is a fascinating character, the adopted daughter of Mayasur – the chief sculptor and architect of the Asuras. Mandodari was as beautiful as she was learned because Mayasur who was very disappointed with his wicked Asura Sons – Mayavi and Dundhubi – had taught Mandodari not only scriptures but engineering and architecture as well. Mandodari used to help him with all his important projects and added just her small feminine touches to make each of his projects a resounding success.

Ravan first met Mandodari, when he went to commission Mayasur's services to design his proposed palace for Shiv in Lanka – it was Ravan's ambition to get his deity, Shiv, to relocate from Kailash to Lanka and the palace had to be grand and incomparable to befit it being Shiv and Parvati's abode. Mayasur called Mandodari. Ravan was immediately smitten with her beauty. However, as the meeting progressed, her knowledge of engineering and architecture and her obvious talent in her vocation, impressed him no end and a firm resolve took shape within him. He knew then that Mandodari was the perfect mate for him and he asked for her hand in marriage. Mayasur declined, knowing that Ravan had a very famous streak of cruelty and arrogance in him. Ravan furious at being denied, drew out his famous

Chandrahaas (sword) and Mandodari intervened and agreed to marry him, knowing that what Ravan wanted, Ravan got! And in any ensuing battle, her father would be no match for the powerful Ravan!

Ravan married her then and there, through the *Gandharva Vivah* rite, and brought her to Lanka. Once married, Mandodari devoted herself totally to him and even went to the Moon to get him the Amrut (Nectar), which the Gods had hidden there after the churning of the ocean. Ravan, in turn, loved Mandodari more than any other queen in his palace, and in some versions of Ramayan, even have him declare in Sita's Swayamvar that if he won the hand of Sita, she would be his queen but never take the place of Mandodari in his life and his heart.

Throughout his later years, when Ravan morphed into a villain, it pained Mandodari that her once talented, knowledgeable husband had degenerated thus into arrogance personified. History is witness to the fact that Mandodari often remonstrated with him, but to no avail. She was worried about him, but her unwavering love towards her husband never changed.

This poem is set at a time when Ravan is dead and Mandodari is left alone with her thoughts. She has to decide, as per the unwritten code of her time, whether she should agree to marry Vibhishan – Ravan's righteous but traitorous younger brother who was set to become the new king of Lanka.

15. Mandodari – on Ravan's Demise

How do I erase your overpowering personality and accept that you are no more,
The handsomest, mightiest, and wisest man I married, whose children I bore?
The world may remember you as Ravan, you will always be my Dashanan,
So learned, you needed ten heads to store your wisdom, not one!

We loved not just each other, but scripture and literature, engineering and architecture,
You cannot die, I went to the moon to bring you that elusive pot of nectar.
And that was my biggest mistake, endowing you with invincibility,
I failed to realise that in the end, absolute power corrupts absolutely!

I watched helplessly as you degenerated into an arrogant, lecherous villain,
Who heeded no advice, respected no counsel and invited destruction!
Now, I see Lanka, your pride and joy, turn into a grieving cemetery,
Even if it means marrying Vibhishan, I will restore it to its former glory!

Vibhishan will have me as his queen and consort, but not our love sublime,
Because a woman loves only once and commits to it for a lifetime!

Sita's Trial by Fire

Prologue

This is the only instance in Ramayan where Lakshman questions one of his elder brother, Ram's decisions. Otherwise, he is known to have completely dedicated his entire life to Ram, whom he idolised. When Ram announces after the war that he will accept Sita only when she walks through fire, ostensibly to prove her chastity, her Agni Pariksha, Lakshman could not bear it anymore!

Let us go back to the time when fourteen years ago, Ram announced his decision to abdicate the throne and proceed to the forests to honour the word given by his father Dashrath to his second wife, Kaikeyi. There was no doubt in Lakshman's mind that he would accompany Ram on his sojourn. He was a little taken aback when Sita also announced that she would accompany Ram as well and he was quite opposed to the idea. What would Sita know of the rigours of forest life? She was a princess and she would find it so difficult to endure the hardships it involved. Women were delicate, and she would just impede their progress and was best left in the palace. But Sita was adamant and Lakshman had to accept that Sita would accompany them to their fourteen-year exile.

Unknown to Lakshman, Sita was Bhumija (daughter of Mother Earth) and adapted herself pretty well to their nomadic existence. She soon endeared herself to Lakshman, by her knowledge of flora and fauna, and by keeping delicious meals ready for the brothers when they were tired from hunting or setting up their households in difficult terrains. She was like a mother figure to Lakshman and she won over her difficult *devar* (brother-in-law) with her tenderness and compassion.

Therefore, when Lakshman heard about the Agni Pariksha, his outburst against Ram was understandable. But then, Ram revealed the real reason behind his demand. Just prior to the abduction of Sita by Ravan, the God of Fire, Agnidev, had had a conference with Ram giving him an idea of what was to follow and Ram had entrusted his beloved Sita to Agnidev who had created her duplicate Maya Sita (Illusionary Sita) or Chhaya Sita (Shadow Sita) who would thereafter accompany Ram and endure all the hardships destined for the original Sita. After Ram's victory, Ram would reclaim the rightful Sita by surrendering Maya Sita to Agnidev, which is why it was important to demand an Agni Pariksha. The advantage of this would be that it would also satisfy the demand of high morality that people of those days expected from their royalty!

The use of Maya (illusion) was practiced quite frequently in warfare as well, for didn't Indrajeet, a master illusionist, create a Maya Sita on the battlefield and kill her publicly to demoralise Ram's army who fell for the illusion, believing that the entire war was futile because Sita for whom the war was fought was already dead?

Therefore, the significance of the line "Only an illusion would fall for another man's illusion" applies equally to Maya Sita falling for the illusion created by Maya Mrig (the illusionary golden deer), or falling prey to the disguise assumed by Ravan as a holy sage to lure Sita out of the Laksman Rekha!

Certain versions of Ramayan also mention Maya Sita to be an incarnation of Vedvati whom Ravan had molested in her previous birth and who had vowed to avenge her humiliation. There are also many texts which state that

Draupadi, who had emerged out of the sacred fire, was actually Maya Sita who had been entrusted to Agnidev who reappears in the Dwapar Yug to assist Lord Vishnu again in his Krishna avatar!

16. Sita's Trial by Fire

Lakshman

Why does my Sita Maiyya have to walk through fire to prove her chastity?

She who shunned Ravan's love and riches and waited for you amid austerity?

My Bhabhi is my mother, she shall not be subject to such immolation,

Is suspicion such a universal emotion or are you after all human?

Ram

Lakshman, how can you even think that I suspect Sita's fidelity?

Sita lives in my heart; doubting her would be doubting my integrity.

Unknown to all, Sita has been entrusted to Agni the Lord of Fire,

Undefiled by Ravan's touch, protected from his lascivious desire.

My real Sita would have seen through Ravan's deception,

Only an illusion will fall for another man's illusion!

Not just my Sita but even Maya Sita is steadfast in my devotion,

But now, the war is over and the time is opportune for our reunion!

Lakshman, no marriage can survive which demands evidence of "purification,"

Because what truly devastates every Sita is not her abduction but Ram's suspicion!

Hanuman's Ramayan

Prologue

This poem centres around Hanuman who was an unbelievable combination of brain and brawn. He had the strength of many thousand elephants and the mere fact that he could uproot an entire mountain and bring it from Himalayas to Sri Lanka is testimony of his sheer might. But apart from that, as an avatar or spiritual son of Shiv (as mentioned in the Shiv Purana), the God of Knowledge – he was very, very knowledgeable. He had mastered the Vedas and all spiritual texts. Lord Ram knew that a better emissary to Ravan could not be found. Add to that his unfailing devotion to Ram and Sita, is it any wonder that Hanuman is worshipped all over the world as God Himself?

His quest for knowledge was so immense that he wanted to master the *Nav Vyakaranas* also which could only be mastered by a *Gruhasth* – a married man. Hanuman was an *Ajanma Brahmachari* (Celibate for life). So, he prayed to his Guru Lord Surya to show him a way out of this dilemma, and Lord Surya created a perfect bride for him from his rays – *Survachal* who was herself an Ajanma Brahmacharini and Lord Surya further blessed him that even after his marriage to Survachal, he could continue to remain celibate.

Hanuman then marries Survachal and masters the last frontier – the Nav Vyakarnas also. Thereafter, though not very well known, he composed the first Ramayan as an epic. During his recital to Lord Ram, Narad was present and he was amazed by the masterpiece. Soon, during his travels, he comes across Valmiki who had also composed his Ramayan and first wanted to take it to Ram, seek his blessings, and then, to the wider audience of the world. Narad informs Valmiki about the sheer brilliance of Hanuman's Ramayan and suggests that rather than going to Lord Ram first, he should take a detour and check out Hanuman's Ramayan.

Valmiki does exactly that and to his consternation, discovers that Narad was right after all, his Ramayan could not hold a candle to Hanuman's Ramayan which was far superior in every parameter. He is almost near tears when Hanuman asks him the reason why and what follows thereafter is captured in the poem.

17. Hanuman's Ramayan

Devrishi Narad to Valmiki

Good though your work is, it is nowhere near Hanuman's epic,

You have not seen his lyric, but I have to be an objective critic.

Compared to his Ramayan, yours seems to be the work of a novice,

Hanuman has poured his heart and soul into it and created a masterpiece!

Valmiki to Hanuman

With awe, Valmiki turned page after page of Hanuman's Ramayan,

He had never seen such a union of prose and poetry, love and emotion,

"If yours becomes public, my Ramayan will only suffer rejection,

Now mine is love's labour lost!' cried Valmiki overcome with dejection!

Hanuman to Valmiki

"I shall destroy it at once if my Ramayan causes you so much misery!"

So saying, Hanuman plunged his tome into the depths of a bottomless sea.

"Mine was created for the Lord and He knows my devotion keen,

Yours is composed for the world, may it be the first, the world has ever seen!"

And to date

It differs from artist to artist, the treatment of their art,

Some crave the world's appreciation, some hold it close to their heart!

From The Mahabharat

Shakuni – His Unspoken Words

Prologue

Among all historical characters, the name Shakuni evokes an image so powerful of villainy, hatred, and conspiracy, the one man who consistently poisoned Duryodhan and Dhritarashtra against Pandavs. Was Shakuni always like this? Circumstances maketh a man – no man is born evil – it is his circumstances which make him so. Even a casual reader of Mahabharat will be prompted to ask – Despite being Gandhar Naresh (King of Gandhar), why did Shakuni never go to Gandhar but stayed in Hastinapur with his sister? How could Gandhari be so righteous and self-sacrificing and her own brother be such an epitome of treachery and deceit?

To answer all these questions and to know Shakuni better, we will have to delve into the past of Saubal (Shakuni's real name), the hundredth son of the King of Gandhar – Subal, the father to a hundred sons and one daughter, Gandhari.

Shakuni loved his sister Gandhari more than anybody else in the whole world and was furious when his father had agreed to give her hand in marriage to the blind prince of Hastinapur – Dhritarashtra. Actually, his father was helpless when Bhishma presented himself with a massive army at the outskirts of Gandhar ostensibly to ask for Gandhari's hand in marriage. The message was clear, either agree to the marriage or face the consequences. The mountainous kingdom of Gandhar had not fought a war in years. Their weapons were rusty and their warriors unused to even minor battles, let alone a war with the mighty Hastinapur army commanded by Bhishma himself.

Worse was to follow because after marriage, Dhritarashtra found out that in order to avert widowhood for Gandhari, as directed by the Gandhar court astrologer, Gandhari had first been married to a goat which had been sacrificed! He was livid at not being the first husband of his wife and was so enraged at this fact being hidden from him, that he once again sent his massive army to capture King Subal and all his hundred sons and ordered their incarceration in Hastinapur's dungeon prisons. For all of King Subal and his hundred sons only one bowl of rice was sent as their daily meal and Subal soon knew that the objective was to starve them to death. Subal then chose his youngest and cleverest son to survive and everybody sacrificed their part of the meal so that Shakuni could survive and exact revenge for all of them.

Day after day, as he saw life ebb out of his ninety-nine brothers, Shakuni's resolve to completely eliminate the Kuru dynasty began to take a firm hold within his psyche but even Subal knew that if Shakuni remained incarcerated all his life, he would never be able to exact revenge. So, King Subal did two important things on his deathbed – he indicated to Dhritarashtra that his last wish was freedom for Shakuni and to Shakuni he requested to make dice out of his bones – these dice would have his spirit in them and would always do Shakuni's bidding. King Subal soon breathed his last and Shakuni was free once more with only two dice and an all-consuming passion for revenge to destroy the entire Kuru dynasty. Shakuni then stabbed himself in his knee so that his limp would forever remind him of his sole purpose in life.

Once free, Shakuni soon realised that odds were insurmountable against him – he had not been to his kingdom for years, he had no army, and traditional warfare would soon see him dead just like his father and brothers – and this is when the crafty and devious Shakuni emerges. Opportunity soon presented itself when he saw Duryodhan and his cousins – the illustrious Pandavs. A plan began to form in his mind. Only the Pandavs could destroy the Kauravs – and he had to somehow bring that about. The brilliant Shakuni soon realized that if he controlled Duryodhan's mind – the vast resources of Hastinapur and the mighty warriors of Hastinapur's army would be under his control. Today, we would call it mind games, Out-of-the-box thinking but Shakuni proved to be a master at it. Shakuni became an expert at Chausar or Chaupat – at throwing the dice so that he always won. One of his little known traits was that he was also a master illusionist. Not only did his prey think what he wanted him to think but they also often saw what Shakuni wanted them to see.

With the barest of resources but an indefatigable will, this poem traces how Shakuni keeps his promise to his dead father and brothers...

18. Shakuni – His Unspoken Words

Dhritrashtra, like my father, you too shall grieve,
On the death of all your hundred sons for as long as you live!
Your merciless torture of my family is imprinted on my broken leg forever,
I shall not rest until I avenge them, every step a painful reminder!

But I know what I was up against, your unconquerable army, warriors and all,
Only a bitter family feud with the mighty Pandavs could cause your downfall.
And so, I began to use treachery and deceit as weapons of mass destruction,
And sowed in your sons' minds, seeds of hate, rivalry, anger, and suspicion!

It bore fruit when Duryodhan, in a game of dice, stripped them of everything,
Unknown to them, my father's soul resided in my dice and always did my bidding.
It bore fruit when Duryodhan refused to part with land, in his words was my voice,
Leading them to self-destruction; war with the Pandavs was actually my choice.

Now on the battlefield, dying, I see carnage and destruction untold,
I smile with satisfaction, isn't revenge a dish best served cold?

To Gandhari – A Few Questions

Prologue

Gandhari's role in history is shrouded in mystery! Nobody ever questioned her piety and virtues, but her decisions have always invited scrutiny and conjecture. History is divided on whether her biggest decision on blindfolding herself prior to entering the royal household of Hastinapur was taken out of undying love and a pledge to share her husband's joys and sorrows equally, or was it an act of rebellion against being married to a blind prince without her consent?

A sneak peek into her past will help.

Gandhari was born to King Subal and Queen Sudharmaa of Gandhar (present day Afghanistan) which was a small mountainous kingdom and she was doted upon by not only her parents but also by her hundred brothers. When Ved Vyas had been the royal guest of Gandhar, she had served him with such dedication that he had blessed her and asked her to seek a boon. The young girl who had seen her parents blessed with a hundred sons, asked for the same. However, of all her brothers, she shared a very special bond with Shakuni, the youngest, who worshipped the ground his sister walked on. Because she was terrified of the dark, every evening, he would gather fireflies for his sister and release them in her chamber at night, so that she would never have to face darkness. What must have prompted Gandhari then to blindfold herself and accept a dark existence for life?

Far away in Hastinapur, when Bhishma heard of a princess with such a boon, he made up his mind that she would be the chosen bride for Dhritrashtra. With a hundred heirs to the royal throne, he would never need to worry about Hastinapur's throne remaining vacant which had come perilously close to having no successor with Vichitravirya's sudden untimely death. So, he set out with his large army for Gandhar and camped on the outskirts of the small country, ostensibly to ask for Gandhari's hand in marriage! The message was clear, either agree to the marriage or face the consequences. Not having fought a war in years, King Subal knew that in any battle with the mighty Hastinapur army, defeat was certain for the mountainous kingdom of Gandhar.

Gandhari knew then that she had no choice in the matter. She would rather have her father accept the alliance than see him routed with many innocent lives lost in what would have been a futile battle. She agreed to get married to Dhritrashtra, however was dismayed when she heard that her future husband was blind! Shakuni was furious, to have his sister being compelled to marry a blind prince who could never get his rightful due of being crowned the king on account of his physical deformity.

This is when she decides to blindfold herself as well and the reasons cited behind this monumental decision are as complex as the decision itself.

- Did she blindfold herself so that she could get first-hand experience of what her blind husband went through every day?
- Did she do it because her marriage vows entailed that she would share all his joys and sorrows equally?
- Did she do it because if men traditionally did not like superior wives, she had willingly forsaken her sight, thus rendering herself as her husband's equal?

- Or did she do it because she was handed a blind husband as a *fait accompli*, so why should her husband have a full bodied wife when she had had to settle for less?

Regardless of her reasons, Dhritrashtra was livid. He had wanted a wife through whose eyes he could see the world. His heart broke at her vow and he never quite forgave Gandhari for this decision of hers.

Eventually, her physical act of blindfolding herself, became symbolic of her turning a blind eye to all of Dhritrashtra's, Shakuni's, and Duryodhan's transgressions of morality, righteousness, though she always urged them to follow the right path. Did she know that this blindfold would eventually make life easy for her, as she did not have to see or bear responsibility as the queen for the reprehensible acts of her husband, her brother, and her sons?

She opened her eyes only once, to grant invincibility to Duryodhan before his combat with Bhim. She is also remembered for her curse to Shakuni, holding him responsible for the war, the utter destruction and the death of all her hundred sons – that his Kingdom shall never see peace again! Current history vouches that this curse has till today proved as potent as when it was uttered 5,000 years ago with Afghanistan – it was called Avgan Sthan (A defective place!) still awaiting peace and harmony.

This sonnet steps into the shoes of the reader, who if opportunity presented itself, would definitely ask these few questions to Gandhari...

19. To Gandhari – A Few Questions

While the Gandhar palace fumed at Bheeshma's unfair alliance,
Gandhari, a dutiful daughter, resigned herself to a blind existence.
After all, she would never have to compete for her blind husband's affection,
There would be no other queen, as long as she accepted his affliction.
And if it is true that a man never really loves a superior wife,
She would accept his blindness and tie a blindfold for life.
The course of history changed in that split second decision,
Gandhari, you lost both, not just your sight but also your vision!

Gandhari, without that blindfold,
You would have seen the bad omens that heralded your first born,
You would have disciplined his villainy and set him on a path of reform.
You would have seen through your family's evil machinations,
You would have singlehandedly changed the destiny of so many nations.

You could have saved a war and a dynasty, Gandhari, did you never realise?
Blessed with a hundred sons, you still died childless – a blindfold at what price?

To Kunti

Prologue

This poem explores the imponderable - what if Kunti had revealed the true story of Karna's birth during the many opportunities she had in her lifetime? How would that revelation have changed the course of history?

Again, it would be necessary to delve a little into the past.

Kunti was born to the Yadav King Shurasen, but was adopted by King Shurasen's childless cousin, Kuntibhoj who changed her original name from Prutha to Kunti. Shurasen was also Vasudev's father and thus, Kunti was aunt to Krishna and the Pandavs were Krishna's first cousins.

Her childhood was quite like the childhood of princesses of the time but a momentous event happened during her youth. Having pleased Sage Durvasa who had come visiting Kuntibhoj's kingdom through her selfless service, he gave her a benediction in the form of a Mantra through which she could call upon any God and receive a child from him. Impulsive as the youth generally are, Kunti invoked the Sun God to test the Mantra and was horrified to receive an exceptionally radiant child in her arms born with a *Kavach* (an armour) and *Kundal* (ear rings) when she wasn't even married! In order to save her family from disrepute and herself from societal scorn, she put the child in a basket and drifted it away in the currents of a river. This child was eventually brought up by the King's charioteer, Adirath, and his wife, Radha, and came to be known as Karna.

As irony would have it, Kunti and Karna's path crossed quite a few times in their lifetimes. In any case, afflicted with Rishi Kadamb's curse, Pandu could have never had children and Kunti did divulge that she knew this unique mantra through which she could beget children from any God she invoked. Pandu exhorted her to use the same and she did it thrice and begot Yudhisthir from Dharmaraja, Bhim from Vayu, and Arjun from Indra. She also allowed Madri to have the benefit of the Mantra and Madri invoked Ashwini Kumars and begot Nakul and Sahadev from them.

So, what stopped her from telling Pandu to first adopt her son Karna and then invoke the mantra to beget children from other Gods? She could have persuaded Pandu to formally adopt him without revealing the whole truth, if that is what she thought appropriate. After all, hadn't Satyavati, her own grand mother-in-law, called her son Ved Vyas from her previous union with Sage Parashar to impregnate Satyavati's daughters-in-law Ambika and Ambalika when their husband Vichitravirya had passed away without giving Hastinapur a heir? That was an opportunity lost!

The second opportunity arose when after Dronacharya announced the completion of formal training of the princes and organized an exhibition match to showcase the prowess of the Kuru and Pandav princes in the art of weaponry. Karna had then walked into the stadium and challenged Arjun in archery! Kunti immediately recognized him from his Kundal and his radiance and fainted briefly and lost yet another opportunity to formally adopt Karna. Had she acted fast then, the entire saga of Duryodhan accepting Karna as his friend and giving him the territory of Anga and thereby elevating his status from Sarathiputra to Anga Raja Karna would have never happened and Karna would have never been in the bondage of gratitude towards Duryodhan for his entire life.

There was yet another opportunity when during Yudhisthir's Ashwamedha Yagna ceremony, when the *Shastraharan* (divesting a warrior of his weapons) of Duryodhan, Karn, and Dushasan was announced, (Refer to Poem no. 30 Duryodhan's Defence) Kunti was alarmed at the turn of events but did nothing and silently witnessed the proceedings.

Just before the war, Kunti, however, confesses to Karna that he is actually the eldest of her children and this is where her image as epitome of maturity, foresight, and dutiful womanhood suffers a little. Why did her heart burn for her five sons and never for Karna who had to suffer a life of ignominy and rejection? How could she, after doing such injustice to him, actually ask him to show mercy towards her children in war? Why hadn't she then revealed the secret to Yudhisthira and begged Arjun and Krishna to spare Karna?

And then, finally, on hearing of Karna's death, she breaks down on the battlefield and reveals the secret to Yudhishthira (refer to Sonnet 27, Yudhishthir's Curse) but by then, the damage was done.

This poem invites the reader to contemplate – how would the course of history have changed if Kunti had revealed this secret much earlier?

20. To Kunti

O Kunti, you recognized Karna as he walked into the competition;
From his earlobes, his armour, and from his radiance of the Sun,
O Kunti, how could you not even make an attempt,
To accept your first born and save him from a lifetime of contempt?

In Draupadi's swayamvar, nobody would have objected to his lineage,
He had all five husbandly qualities Draupadi desired in a marriage.
The ethical code of a sage, a warrior, and an unparalleled archer,
The mightiest, the handsomest, of undoubted regal composure!

Later, when Pandavas returned and demanded their kingdom,
Your acceptance of Karna would have rejected war as the only option.
As in the past, Duryodhan would have gladly gifted land to his friend,
With Yudhishthir's acceptance, all hostilities would have to end.

You failed Kunti, to avoid infamy, to keep Karna's birth a mystery,
Because you are still remembered as the first unwed mother in history!

Draupadi's Dilemma

Prologue

Whilst Arjun's moral dilemma on the battlefield of Kurukshetra and Lord Krishna's exposition of the Geeta are extremely well documented, researched, and commented upon, another major moral dilemma that the Pandavs and Draupadi faced has been glossed over completely in the recounting of the Mahabharat. This arose when after winning Draupadi's hand, Arjun brings her home and announces to Mother Kunti that he had brought alms home that day which could be considered as a special bounty! Without turning back, Kunti, as was her wont, advised the Pandavs to share this equally among them!

With this casual utterance, it was as though the assembly of Pandavs and Draupadi had been struck by a sudden thunderbolt! Pandavs brought up on the highest principles of Dharma, including obeying without dissent all commands from their parents, were aghast at what obedience with this particular mandate entailed! Imagine the plight of Draupadi as a new bride, the princess of Panchal, married to a Brahmin instead of a Kshtariya prince, being asked to walk miles in the harsh sunlight to the humble abode of the Brahmins, located on the outskirts of the city and much worse than physical discomfort was the morally abhorrent thought that she was to be shared as a wife by five brothers!

Whilst history relegates this predicament to a summary statement, that Pandavs accepted their mother's mandate as a fait accompli, truth was far from this. Each of the five brothers was deeply tormented and anguished by the very thought, Bhim, as usual, was the first to voice his agony – all his life he had been taught to treat his elder brother's wife akin to his mother and his younger brother's wife akin to his daughter. How could he even bring himself to contemplate conjugal relations with them? The ever righteous Yudhisthir, thought that even such thoughts and Mother Kunti's blasphemous utterance had made them unfit to ever look at Draupadi in the eye again or as much live in the same palace with her. And all of them were unanimous that they could not subject the Princess of Panchal to such an unjust fate.

Finally, Yudhisthir decided that since Arjun had won her hand in the Swayamvar, he would be the only one who would marry her and the others had no option but to renounce the world and live the life of ascetics and practise celibacy for the rest of their lives. Arjun was adamant that Draupadi should be married to the eldest brother, Yudhisthir, so that the dynasty could continue and beget an heir apparent to Hastinapur's throne. They finally, asked Draupadi (by then they had revealed to her that they were not Brahmins but the Pandav princes!) to choose between the suggested options!

Draupadi was aghast at all the options. Yudhisthir and Bhim both were elder to Duryodhan but Arjun was not and whilst she would prefer to be married to Arjun, she could not bring about herself to be the cause of Duryodhan being declared the King of Hastinapur. This would be a certain eventuality if both Yudhisthir and Bhim were to forever renounce the world and accept a nomadic existence! And she knew that Mother Kunti would never smile again holding herself guilty for relegating her mighty children to ascetism. Without doubt, this would forever cast a gloom on her married life with Arjun. Though having emerged from fire, Draupadi had never anticipated such a fire test of herself and she made a decision befitting a queen and a daughter-in law, that she would obey her mother-in-law and marry all five Pandavs!

This was not an easy decision for her or the Pandavs. Ved Vyas counselled the Pandavs and Draupadi beset with self doubt and derision turned to her best friend Lord Krishna to guide her forward! This poem captures the conversation between Draupadi and Krishna in the above background of events, but this was not the end of this matter.

Krishna consoles her in his inimitable manner, reminds her how in her previous birth as Nalayani, she had sought from Shiv the boon of a husband who would be the most righteous, the strongest, the best archer, the handsomest, and the calmest. Shiv had objected saying that it was impossible to get all these qualities in one man but Nalayani had persisted with Shiv until Shiv exasperatedly told her she would have to marry five men if she wanted all the above qualities. This was but a manifestation of that boon. Perhaps, Draupadi's life is a sterling example of 'be careful of what you wish, lest you get it.'

Krishna also blesses his Sakhi with unblemished chastity, and even her public disrobing does not take away from the fact that her chastity remained unsullied. Draupadi was also blessed with Aajeevan Kaumarya (lifelong virginity) which ironically helped her considerably when she was married to five men.

Further to the decision of Draupadi marrying all five Pandavs, a code of conduct was evolved whereby Draupadi would spend one year exclusively with one husband by rotation and any brother entering her chamber when she was supposed to be with another brother had to undergo exile for 12 years. At the end of that one year, Draupadi who had emerged from fire would take an Agnisnan (a fire bath) where her virginity would be restored for her next husband. So, within her polyandrous existence, at any given point of time, Draupadi was monogamous and, therefore, to date, she is revered as one of the Panchkanyas – the most respected chaste women of all times with the other 4 being Ahilya, Sita, Mandodari, and Tara.

21. Draupadi's Dilemma

Draupadi to Krishna

Sakha, Arjun and I cannot enjoy wedded bliss built on the family's misery,
Our marriage cannot mean for all his brothers a lifetime of ascetism and celibacy!
Without Yudhisthir and Bhima, on Hastinapur's throne would be Duryodhan,
Which outcome has to be averted, however unpalatable the final solution!
Govind, I have no choice, but to marry all five brothers, albeit unconventional,
But I am pained, that posterity will always think of me as highly immoral!

Krishna

If a decision is good for your new family, your kingdom, and people at large,
Sakhi, how can it be tainted with an immoral and a repugnant charge?
Draupadi, this is all ordained by destiny even Kunti's uncharacteristic utterance,
A denouement of your unreasonable boons and their unwelcome consequence.
Do not fight your destiny because this will lead to averting a larger calamity,
History will always remember you as a symbol of virtue and unblemished chastity.

And it follows to date
That a desperate solution may be necessitated to combat a desperate time,
Just as killing is heroic in war, but otherwise a reprehensible crime!

Yudhishthir Prashna
(Questions to Yudhishthir)

Prologue

This poem captures one of the most erudite conversations of our ancient history and has been recorded as Yudhishthir *Prashna* or Yudhishthir *Baka* (Crane) *Upakhyan* and happens when the Pandavs are just entering their twelfth year of incognito exile.

Whilst setting out on their journey towards the kingdom that was supposed to be their incognito domicile for the next one year, on the path, Yudhishthir gets very thirsty and the Pandavs realise that their stock of water was depleted. Sahadev climbs up a tree and spots a lake in the distance, and offers to go and fetch some water from the lake. When he gets close to the lake, a crane appears and warns him against taking some water from the lake without seeking permission first and answering some of his questions, failing which the water would turn into poison. Sahadev ignored him and no sooner did he drink the water, he fell down dead by the edge of the lake. One by one all his brothers, save and except Yudhishthir, met with the same fate and finally, it fell on Yudhishthir to go in search of his brothers and water.

He soon came to the lake and saw his brothers lying lifeless, without any vestige of a battle or any injury on their bodies. Parched as he was, he decided to drink some water first, but the same crane appeared before him and Yudhishthir realized, that this was no mere mortal, but a celestial being who had felled his mighty brothers without a battle. He then decided to pay his respects and answer the questions put to him by the Yaksha, who manifested himself in front of Yudhishthir.

For all of us who get anxious watching the contestants on reality quiz shows, think of Yudhishthir in the hot seat with the stake of his own and his brothers' lives hanging by the mere thread of the correctness of his answers! Yaksha asks him a staggering 126 questions on topics ranging from sociology, biology, metaphysics, astronomy, et al.

In order to fit into my 14-line sonnet, I have picked up 5 of my favourite questions by Yaksha and Yudhishthir's answers to the same.

When Yudhishthir answered all of Yaksha's questions correctly, Yaksha revealed his true identity that he was actually his father Dharmaraja (Lord Yama from whom Kunti had begotten Yudhishthir) and asked him to choose any one of his brothers who could be brought back to life again! Whom does Yudhishthir choose? Not the world's best archer, Arjun; nor the mighty Bhim but Nakul! The last question that Dharmaraja asked him was to explain his choice and Yudhishthir's reply revealed a thought process that places justice and equity before other considerations.

This sonnet is a mere glimpse into the rapid fire rounds that Yaksha as a quiz master subjected Yudhishthir to and his final reward at clearing all rounds with his carefully thought through and well-reasoned answers. The sonnet follows the same pattern, questions by Yaksha, answers by Yudhishthir and the last couplet is the reward for an outstanding performance.

22. Yudhishthir Prashna

You dare not partake of my lake's water without answering my questions first,
See the fate of your defiant brothers who attempted to quench their thirst!

I apologise for the folly of my brothers who disregarded your warning,
I pay obeisance to you and shall answer to my best, O celestial being!

So, tell me, what grows faster than grass? The worries of a man;
And what travels faster than wind? A human mind definitely can!

How does one synergise contrary needs of ethics, profit, and desire in one's life?
One can easily harmonise all three by acquiring a beautiful, dutiful wife!

What in this world causes the biggest surprise, the most wonder?
That man who sees death all around, still wishes to live forever!

When granted the boon of one life, why did you choose Nakul, my son?
Kunti's eldest had to choose Madri's eldest, that is the only righteous decision!

Yudhishthir, I am blessing you with the life of all your brothers and success true,
Because you truly combine knowledge, intelligence and wisdom with respectful virtue!

Vidur's Choice

Prologue

This poem is set on Vidur from Mahabharat – one of ancient India's greatest royal advisors, a brilliant statesman, a firm believer and practitioner of a strict code of morality and ethics and also the author of Vidur Niti which thousands of years later, inspired yet another well-known treatise - Chanakya Niti.

Vidur was the earthly avatar of Yamaraj or Dharmaraja, living out his human existence under a curse from Sage Mandavya who was enraged on finding that Yamaraj had caused him to suffer punishment hugely disproportionate to his juvenile sin. Sage Mandavya cursed Dharmaraj to be born as a human, not as a privileged royal but born to a *shudra* so he understands first-hand the compulsions of a human existence which he was wont to judge and mete out harsh punishments to.

Coming back to the Kuru dynasty, it had so transpired that Vichitravirya had died leaving his two wives without any children and Hastinapur without a successor to the royal throne. Queen Satyavati, then commanded Ved Vyas, her own son from a previous marriage and the half-brother of Vichitravirya to impregnate his two queens, Ambika and Ambalika. Terrified at the external demeanour of the unkempt, ungroomed hirsute sage, Ambika closed her eyes and Ambalika turned ashen pale during their time with Ved Vyas. Vyas duly reported this to the Queen Satyavati, cautioning that their children would be afflicted with representative maladies (Dhritarashtara was born blind and Pandu pale) and so, the Queen Satyavati ordered Ambika to try once more – but this time, Ambika sent her maid Parishrami or Shudri to Ved Vyas. Shudri was neither repelled nor terrified by his appearance and gave birth eventually to a wise, strong, and brilliant Vidur.

Though born to a Shudra mother, he was given a royal upbringing and was quite a favourite with Bhishma Pitamaha for his native intelligence and his expertise in wielding all weapons, the sword in particular. On Pandu's death, when Dhritarashtra took over as caretaker king, Vidur remained his trusted minister and Hastinapur flourished under his governance, until later, when he got undermined once Duryodhan came of age.

Vidur was also one of the staunchest devotees of Lord Krishna and his mansion soon became the abode of choice for Kunti (who would not live with the royal family after Draupadi's dishonour and Pandavs' exile) and for Krishna, when he came as a peace emissary from the Pandavs before the great war. As a mark of affection, Krishna had also gifted him one of the most powerful bows of the time, the Govarthan, the use of which guaranteed the user victory over his enemy.

Perhaps subconsciously, or because he was aware of his low lineage, Vidur always expressed his opinions covertly using veiled references – his most famous covert advice to Yudhishthir was before Yudhishthir left for *Varnavrat* with his mother and brothers – "Remember, Yudhishthir, the only creatures who escape forest fires are snakes and rodents because they use subterranean refuges!"

The only time he used strong emphatic language in his life time was when just before the war, Lord Krishna had come to Hastinapur (on Vidur's insistence) and Duryodhan not only rejected the peace offer but announced in a fit of rage and arrogance that he would not part with land, forget five villages, not even as much as could be accommodated on the tip of a needle! Not satisfied with this, he ordered his guards to take Lord Krishna captive and imprison him.

This poem is set in that explosive atmosphere at the royal court of Hastinapur, and hopefully, brings alive that conversation from our ancient history and explains why in the end Vidur walks away from it all and chooses to go on a pilgrimage instead.

23. Vidur's Choice

Vidur to Dhritarashtra

I beseech you, O King, for once, do not listen to your son, Duryodhan,
For now he seems to be the worst enemy of your dynasty and nation!
He has crossed all limits, by ordering the incarceration of a peace emissary,
Surely, for Hastinapur, this portends untold destruction and endless misery!

Duryodhan to Vidur in a thunderous rage

You should be ashamed of your seditious effrontery and the advice you just gave,
Which minister asks his King to surrender territory, except the coward son of a slave!
Neither my kingdom nor my army needs your ill meaning counsel,
Your love for Pandavas brands you forever as a traitor and an infidel!

A resigned Vidur to the Assembly

Since the King is silent, to the wishes of the Crown Prince I must abide,
I walk away from the war that will bring with it annihilation and homicide!
I beg forgiveness from my ancestors as I lay my beloved Govarthan at your door,
I cannot bring myself to be a party or a witness to this destruction anymore!

And thus, Vidur Niti teaches us, against injustice to raise our dissenting voice,
But when impossible odds overwhelm us, walking away is also a choice!

The Warrior Who Walked Away

Prologue

My readers will experience a sense of deja vu because this is a sequel to my earlier poem Vidur's choice and talks of another notable warrior of those times, who chose not to participate in the Mahabharat war but decides to go on a pilgrimage instead. Another great warrior of those times who also walks away without participating in the war, was the mighty warrior Balram, Krishna's elder brother and reincarnation of Sheshnag.

Throughout their childhood, Krishna and his *Dau* (elder brother in popular lingo) were inseparable and Balram had always been at Krishna's side through the numerous wars they fought in order to establish their Dwarka – the Yadav kingdom. Balram was a mighty warrior himself and was so good at wielding the mace that he had coached both Bhim and Duryodhan in mace combat. Duryodhan proved to be a better pupil unlike Bhim who often relied on brute strength to win, and under the watchful eyes of Balram, Duryodhan mastered the fine art of wielding a mace in terms of strategy and psychological warfare as well. Balram so doted on Duryodhan that he promised the hand of Subhadra, his beloved sister, in marriage to Duryodhan, not realizing that Subhadra had already set her heart on Arjun. He was livid when he heard that Arjun had abducted Subhadra, but Krishna soon pacified him by telling him the truth – actually

Subhadra was the charioteer of the chariot supposedly used for her "abduction," so technically, she was the abductor.

This poem is set when war between the Kauravs and Pandavs seemed inevitable, and both sides were preparing for war in earnest. It was important for both sides to persuade all the reigning kings to be their allies in this all-important war, but none more important than the kingdom of Dwarka under Krishna, who in all important matters, consulted his Dau (Balram). Getting Dau on their side could mean eventual victory or defeat and both sides found themselves face to face with Dau together!

Duryodhan had been primed by Shakuni to play his underdog card – (Balram was known to favour underdogs), how he had been gypped out of his kingdom just because his father was blind, how his wedding procession had to return empty handed, without the bride because Subhadra had been abducted by Arjun. Balram sees through that and gives him a fitting reply.

He does not even spare Arjun and does not allow him to take the moral high stand of ethics, morality, or religion and in no uncertain terms castigates Yudhishthir's mindless interpretation of Kshatriya Dharm which demanded that a true Kshatriya never turns down a challenge from another Kshatriya to play *Chausar/Chaupat* or fight a battle

And this is where Balram wins the heart of all future generations by decrying the conduct of Yudhishthir who commits the unpardonable sin of gambling his wife away and subjecting her to the worst humiliation ever suffered by any queen in history! In fact, he is quite scathing when he tells Arjun that the worse sinner among Yudhishthir and Duryodhan was unquestionably Yudhisthir, thus echoing the sentiments of all of modern India reading the epic almost 5,000 years later who find Yudhisthir's conduct deplorable and heinous! Balram proves himself to be a man of quiet physical strength, and of a balanced mental outlook, the only warrior and king of that era who had the courage and conviction of speaking his mind and forging his own path without giving into false compulsions.

This, when he was Sheshnag to his Vishnu, thus once again proves that mortals have many dilemmas unknown to their celestial counterparts! This poem captures the conversation Balram had with both Duryodhan and Arjun and justifies his decision of not participating in the war! His impassioned plea at the end proved quite prophetic because even the victors inherited only bereavement (the Pandavs lost all their sons!) and a nation of grieving widows, destitute parents, and orphaned children.

24. The Warrior Who Walked Away

Balram to Duryodhan

How can you complain of injustice, when Pandavas have been in exile,
And you have not given up even a day of your decadent lifestyle?
Subhadra was promised to you when I had not known of her preference,
In fact, Pandavas have suffered, because Hastinapur is their rightful inheritance.

Balram to Arjun

Your misdeeds have brought you all to such dire straits, you do realise,
Yudhishthir gambled away his kingdom, brothers, and wife to the spin of dice,
To what false sense of duty or religion did he owe such a mistaken allegiance?
Pandavs have committed the worst sin, redeemable by no amount of penitence!

Balram to both

Duryodhan, you want this war to satisfy your insatiable greed to be the emperor,
Arjun, you want to reverse the events of the recent past and reclaim your honour,
So, you will plunge your innocent subjects into bloodshed for an unnecessary show of might,
I declare, I shall not participate in this war because none of you is right!

Can't you see, it is only futility and anguish that a family feud can bring,
When brother fights brother, even the victor loses everything!

Draupadi – The Angst of a Mother

Prologue

Draupadi who emerged out of fire, remains one of the strongest characters of Mahabharat, from the time she emerges from fire till the time the Pandavs win the war and she is reigning empress again. Popular folklore has strengthened the impression that Draupadi wanted to avenge her humiliation at the hands of Duryodhan, Dushashan, and, therefore, kept the flames of revenge burning within the Pandavs' hearts. Whilst this was true to a certain extent, as the events began to unfold and talks of war grew in scale and intensity, her disquiet grew and she began to have second and third thoughts.

Initially, she had been so confident of the prowess and the battlefield supremacy of her husbands that she saw no downside to the war. In her mind, her husbands would emerge victorious, their kingdom would be restored to them, she would be the reigning empress again, and her insults in the Royal Court of Hastinapur would be avenged with the blood of her tormentors. Before departing for the forests to finish their exile, she had entrusted her sons to her father King Drupad in Panchal, where they had been brought up under the care of Shikhandi, her sister and Dhrishtadyumna her brother. Once the Pandav exile and incognito year had ended she had been reunited with them, nothing had given her more pleasure to see what fine lads the five princes had grown up into.

She was also looking forward to Abhimanyu's wedding with Uttara. Finally, after many years of hardship, it seemed that Gods of fortune and happiness were smiling on her again and yes, they would have to fight the war, but from then onwards, she would let nothing mar her hard-earned happiness! So, she was shocked when the queen of Virat Kingdom, Queen Sudeshna, confided in her that despite her initial misgivings about allowing Uttara to marry Abhimanyu, she had been reassured by Krishna that it would be Uttara's son who was destined to be the monarch of the whole *Aryavrat*.

Draupadi was shocked – all her sons, Prativindhya (Yudhishthir's son), Shutasom (Bhim's son), and the sons of Arjun, Nakul, and Sahadev were older than Abhimanyu – who was actually sixth in the line to the throne – then, why would Abhimanyu's son rule over Aryavrat, unless…unless… her natural born children died even before producing any heir! This was a horrifying thought and she could not resist running to her best friend, Krishna, for reassurance. On her relentless prodding, Krishna confided in her that the only survivors from the entire Pandav dynasty would be the five Pandavs themselves and the war would demand the sacrifice of all other descendants except the one who would still be unborn (but conceived) at the time of the war.

Draupadi was devastated and the dialogue that happens between Krishna and herself is captured in the following sonnet!

25. Draupadi: The Angst of a Mother

Draupadi

Krishna, I beseech you, I do not want war, this total annihilation,

Let it never be said that Draupadi was the cause of this untold destruction.

I will live with my shame, for it is not mine alone.

I cannot sacrifice my children to make a civilization atone.

I want mortal pleasures as well of growing old with my progeny,

Govind, I plead, allow me to choose peace over war as my destiny.

Krishna

Sakhi, you are no ordinary mortal, this is not why you evolved,

You are my most potent weapon, the firmness of your husbands' resolve.

Today, when civilisation's most valiant gatekeepers have chosen vice over virtue,

We must unshackle religion from blind tradition and restore a world order new.

Isn't it enough for you that the Lord Himself is seeking your assistance?

Sakhi, do not resist war, for that is the true purpose of your existence.

Sakhi, war is the only outcome for a civilization so steeped in sin,

Go forth and be the catalyst that will make it implode from within!

Krishna's Invisible Presence

Prologue

Krishna and Arjun – the Dwapar Yug manifestation of Narayan and Nar respectively were best friends, first cousins (Arjun's mother Kunti was Krishna's father, Vasudev's sister) and brothers-in-law (Krishna's sister Subhadra was married to Arjun). There was obviously a very thick bond between the two! Through Mahabharat, Arjun's valour and bravery remain undisputed but many of his victories could not have been achieved without the presence of Krishna by his side, especially during his toughest challenges.

This sonnet captures two such challenges which were defining elements in Mahabharat – one was Draupadi's swayamvar where Krishna prevails upon a reluctant Arjun to walk up and accept the challenge – Krishna's role here was all encompassing – he persuaded Drupad to host a swayamvar for Draupadi and keep a feat in archery (Arjun's forte) for Draupadi's hand in marriage as a winning stake. He persuaded the incognito Pandavas to participate in the swayamvar and Arjun to win Draupadi's hand in marriage. Though to the world, it was and still is Arjun's excellent display of archery, but apart from these known facts, Krishna's special contribution to Arjun's success is captured in the sonnet.

The second occasion is the last battle between Karna and Arjun – Karna whose lifetime ambition was to defeat Arjun in war, was fighting like a man possessed, like someone who had nothing to lose – Krishna knew that and used all his divinity to protect Arjun! Once, Krishna sunk his chariot six inches into the ground to deflect an arrow invoked by Karna aimed at Arjun's neck, but could only strike Arjun's crown and thus save him. The last battle was so fierce that at both sides, war was suspended because their troops could not take their gaze away from the mighty battle being fought between Karna and Arjun.

At every display of valour from Karna's end, Krishna was very vocal in his admiration for Karna and this hurt Arjun immeasurably – so after the battle when Karna was killed, Arjun asked Krishna about his open appreciation for the enemy. This sonnet captures that conversation as well and once again, highlights the role Krishna played during the war, though right till the end, he never wielded a single weapon. It also reiterates a powerful lesson that no matter how accomplished you are, without His presence and blessings, victory is not possible.

26. Krishna's Invisible Presence

At Draupadi's swayamvar, Krishna to Arjun

Parth, hold your breath and hand steady, and focus on the water below;
To unerringly strike the eye of the rotating fish above with your arrow,
And to answer your unspoken question as to how I will help you,
Parth, I will do the impossible and keep the water still for you!

At Kurukshetra after Karna's death, Arjun to Krishna

Madhav, I have surpassed him weapon for weapon, blow for blow,
And yet, you have praise only for a dead and defeated Karna's arrow,
His arrows could hardly move ours, but mine sunk his chariot into the grounds,
Madhav, for an enemy like him, how come in your heart only respect abounds?

Krishna to Arjun

Parth, your chariot has the Lord in it and on top Hanuman's flag,
Praise be to him, despite this, our chariot, he could still push back,
And burn to ashes, it is only my presence which has kept it intact,
After you, when I alight, you will see the wreckage in fact!

And thus, like Arjun,
It is God's invisible presence that pulls us through life's toughest hardships,
Whilst He does not promise us stormless seas, He does ensure unsinkable ships!

Yudhisthir's Curse

Prologue

The Mahabharat war was coming to an end. The last remaining mighty warrior, Karna, had been killed and the Pandavs' victory was a forgone conclusion. As was their nightly routine, the Pandavs were walking through the battlefield, giving medical aid to their injured but still alive, soldiers and arranging for the funeral rites of those who had achieved martyrdom in the war. Suddenly, they saw Kunti, their mother, on the battlefield, cradling their sworn enemy Karna's head in her lap and crying profusely. They were shocked. Karna was their enemy; he was the weapon in Duryodhan's arsenal on whom Duryodhan had depended to wreak injustice and atrocities. It was unbelievable that their own mother should grieve so much over his death.

Yudhisthir could not take it anymore, and along with his brothers, he demanded an explanation from Kunti on her strange behaviour. Still crying profusely, Kunti, for the first time, publicly acknowledged that Karna was her son, gifted to her by Surya before matrimony, and also revealed that though Karna had the ability to slay all Pandavs easily except Arjun who was the only one among them to stand up to him in valour, he had promised Kunti that even if opportunity presented itself on the battlefield, he would not kill any other Pandav except Arjun. With Arjun, it would be a fight to the finish – either Arjun would survive or Karna would – but Kunti's count of her five sons would remain undisturbed. True to his promise, till his death, he did not kill any of the other Pandavs, though he had them at his mercy by divesting them of weapons in his individual combat with each of them! This poem narrates the story of Kunti revealing her secret, Yudhisthir's torment on hearing it, and his curse on women through the ages!

27. Yudhisthir's Curse

Kunti

This warrior on whose death you are rejoicing is actually your elder brother,
And I, who could never publicly accept him, am his ill-fated mother!
You owe your lives to him, he spared you even when he was the enemy,
Mother, you shall always have your five sons, was his promise to me!

Yudhisthir

Every unbelievable word of yours is causing me untold anguish from inside,
My entire life of piety and morality has now been sullied by fratricide,
All through his lifetime, we have cruelly heaped on him scorn and injustice,
Further shame on us, even his death has been caused by trickery and artifice!

Just by revealing the truth, you could have averted war and changed destinies,
Your secret led to this carnage, Mother, when you could have chosen peace!
And if such are the consequences of keeping secrets, I curse all womankind,
Henceforth, she shall never be able to keep any fact private in her mind!

To this date
Blurting out secrets is second nature to women, a compulsive obsessive disorder,
And if they are forced to keep them, it destroys their peace and sanity forever!

An Enigma Called Karna

Prologue

This poem is set in the backdrop of Karna's death and the subsequent discovery of the Pandavas that Karna was actually Kaunteya (Kunti's son) and not Radheya (Radha's son) and that the brave warrior they had always considered their sworn enemy was actually their elder brother. Yudhisthir particularly was so grief stricken that he was talking of renunciation and this was affecting the other four Pandavas as well. Krishna then enlightened the Pandavas about the enigmatic Karna – his past birth, which explained why Karna always seemed a contradiction in terms – morally righteous but Duryodhan's ally, brave and courageous but used his valour knowingly for the wrong reasons, respectful of women but hurled the worst abuse at Draupadi...

Krishna explained that in his past birth, Karna was an Asura called Dambhodbhava, who had performed the most rigorous penance of Lord Surya and was entitled to a boon. Like most asuras of his time, he sought immortality but Lord Surya asked him to settle for anything else – Gods could not grant immortality to anybody. Dambhodbhava then put up a very cunning request to Surya to bless him with a 1000 armours – each such that it would take a 1000 years of penance for anybody to shatter even one and whoever succeeded met with instant death. (The average lifespan in Satyug was a hundred thousand years!)

This boon was granted and blessed with such immense powers, Dambhodbhava unleashed a reign of terror until he met his match in Nar and Narayan (twin sages, who were later reborn as Arjun and Krishna respectively in Dwapar Yug). Nar and Narayan were devotees of Shiv and had imbibed mastery over warfare and scriptures from Lord Shiv Himself. They had the power to invoke the *Mahamrityunjaya mantra* (granted to somebody who had done a rigorous penance of a 1000 years) which could bring the dead back to life again! So, Nar and Narayana then took turns at shattering the armours of Dambhodbhava – as soon as one armour was shattered by Nar, he would die but Narayan would invoke the Mahamrityunjaya mantra and bring him to life again who continued his meditation – in the meantime, Narayan fought Dambhodbhava and broke his armour and died instantly but Nar revived him and continued the fight. Thus, 999 armours were shattered and when it came down to the last armour, Dambhodbhava fled for his life and sought refuge in his deity, Lord Surya, who sheltered him. Narayan who was chasing him then, was so enraged that he cursed him to be born as human when Nar and Narayan would kill him finally.

But because he was in Surya's refuge when this happened, Dambhodbhava carried Surya's divine lineage as well in his next birth as Karna who was born with that one last armour and Kundal.

Therefore, it was not just paternal love that Indra had for Arjun which made him seek Karna's armour from him before the war, it was to save Arjun from instant death when in the war, he would finally kill Karna – because if Karna would have been killed with the armour on, killing Karna would have meant instant death for Arjun as well! Krishna's explanation to the Pandavas is the setting for this poem.

28. An Enigma Called Karna

Krishna to the Pandavs

Grieve not, O Pandavs, for the loss of your elder brother,
Even Karna could not escape his karma, as you will soon discover!
Born as Dambhodbhava, he performed rigorous penance and sought immortality,
When denied, he asked for a thousand armours to guard himself from fatality!

For many aeons, Nar and Narayana took turns in shattering his 999 armours,
Until he ran to Lord Surya for refuge and foiled them in their last endeavour!
Surya shielded him and an enraged Narayan cursed him to be born as human again,
The sins of his last birth have resulted in him suffering so much injustice and pain.

Thus was born Karna, with his last invincible Kavach and Kundal,
A rare combination of a vicious Asura and Surya, divine and noble!
The demon in him caused Draupadi's insult and Abhimanyu's death,
The God in him made him charitable and brave till his last breath.

Thus to date,
Even after centuries, Karna's life and times fascinate and hold us enthralled,
Because aren't we all like him, part God, part devil, and human after all?

Uddhav's Debate

Prologue

The first question that my readers will seek an answer to it is - Who was Uddhav?

Uddhav was Krishna's best friend and first cousin – Uddhav's father was Devbhanga – Vasudev's elder brother but just as Krishna's friendship with Arjun (his first cousin on the maternal side) was legendary, so was his friendship with Uddhav (his first cousin on the paternal side). Just as he imparted his teachings to Arjun in Geeta, so he imparted his teachings to Uddhav in Uddhav Geeta or Hansa Geeta!

Uddhav was the first Yadav to offer his friendship to Krishna when he came to Mathura (this was just before the slaying of Kans and his valour was yet to be established) and two more different friends could not be found. Uddhav was an urbane and a knowledgeable man and had a deep understanding of the scriptures, and Krishna was a cowherd who was known more for romancing the milkmaids with his flute. But Uddhav sensed the divinity within Krishna and Krishna sensed the righteousness and the erudition of Uddhav and they soon became very firm friends. After the slaying of Kans, Krishna's destiny led him to the fulfilment of onerous duties and he knew that his days with Radha and his *Gopis (milkmaids)* were now a thing of the past. But Radha and the Gopis were waiting for his return and he knew he could not have found a more composed, learned emissary than Uddhav for breaking the news to the grief-stricken Radha and Gopis - that Krishna would never return to Vrindavan again.

Uddhav sets out on this mission with a slightly condescending attitude – if they were very distraught, he would teach them detachment, the deeper meanings of their lives and duties and he would quote from various scriptures and vedas to prove his point. These were after all rural women and he would be patient with them. Reality, of course, turns out to be quite different and the Gopis with their absolute devotion, end up teaching Uddhav more – he stayed back six months at Vrindavan because he found their infinite love a revelation – they ended up teaching him Bhakti Yog instead of learning Gyan Yog from him. Therein also lies Uddhav's greatness – when he found a path completely different from what he had chosen, he still stayed back to completely grasp what were ideas he would probably have laughed at back in Mathura.

Uddhav comes back to a great friendship with Krishna as he becomes Krishna's trusted companion in peace and charioteer in the many battles Krishna had to fight to establish his Yadav Kingdom with Dwarka (the city with eight gates) as its capital.

This poem is set after the coronation of Yudhishthir at Hastinapur post the defeat of the Kauravs at Kurukshetra and Krishna realizes that it was time for him to end his avatar and return to *Vaikunth* – so, one day, when they were sitting together, Krishna asks Uddhav to seek a boon from him because Uddhav had never sought anything at all from him until then. A man of immense knowledge and learning, Uddhav declines a boon but demands explanations! There were many things about the recent past that had puzzled him about Krishna's conduct – but how do you hold God accountable? When Krishna permits him to ask as many questions as he needs to until he is completely satisfied, Uddhav sets out on this discovery into Krishna's psyche, his compulsions, and his thought process. The result enriches him more than any boon ever could have.

This poem brings a glimpse into that illuminating conversation which God has with His firm devotee and questioning friend and when Krishna, in justifying his conduct, brings the philosophy of karma into it, Uddhav becomes sarcastic – surely God can play a role in preventing sin rather than punishing people later for their bad karma? Krishna's one-liner is a fitting reply to that sarcasm and is a pointer towards the distance we have created between God and ourselves when we judge our daily conduct in that context.

29. Uddhav's Debate

Uddhav to Krishna

If a friend in need is a friend indeed, and you the epitome of friendship,
How could you have put your best friends Pandavs through so much hardship?
You could have stopped Yudhishthir in time, you were omniscient and knew everything,
Or helped Draupadi, after all her dishonour had started much before her disrobing!

Krishna to Uddhav

Yudhishthir knew of my disapproval to his acceptance of the gambling invitation,
And he had forbidden me to enter the assembly until my invocation!
Duryodhan was smarter, he had asked Shakuni to play on his behalf,
If Yudhishthir had asked me to play, who would have had the last laugh?

Each of the brothers cursed their fate, but me they failed to call!
When every warrior, elder failed Draupadi, she invoked me last of all,
Draupadi delayed; not me, but , remember, if karma ordains a suffering true,
Gods are also helpless because that's when wisdom deserts the wisest too!

Lord, shouldn't then God stop His devotees from bad karma of piling sin upon sin?
Uddhav, Shouldn't then devotees refrain from vice, knowing that God is watching?

Duryodhan's Defence

Prologue

The character of Duryodhan remains vivid in our memory as a villain; arrogant, vindictive, and insanely jealous, who plunged millions into war, as he adamantly refused all peace overtures from Krishna as the emissary of Pandavs. But if Duryodhan was ever given an opportunity to defend himself and answer to the many charges against him, what would his pleading look like? This sonnet goes into the imaginary realm of Duryodhan being given a chance to explain his conduct, and in order to do so, he takes us into his past at the events which unfolded right from his childhood.

Duryodhan, the eldest son of Dhritrashtra, was born in very unusual circumstances indeed. After an incubation of nearly 2 years, Gandhari delivered a cold lump of flesh which was cut up into 101 pieces and stored in earthen urns filled with ghee. Indeed the time of Duryodhan emerging from the urn as a newborn was accompanied with so many ominous signs, wolves baying, dogs howling, and the entire universe being engulfed by the most impenetrable darkness, that the court astrologers advised the King to kill his new born son! But on being assured that the infant was healthy in all respects born without any physical deformity, Dhritrashtra and Gandhari would not hear of it!

They lavished their first born with all the luxuries that mark a royal childhood and Duryodhan always believed that one day, (his desire duly fanned by Shakuni), he would ascend the Hastinapur throne. He was, therefore, not prepared at all, when suddenly fate brought his cousins from the forest, to be his equals and the virtuous Pandavs soon won the hearts of the royal household and Hastinapur's subjects. Even as kids, he had many times observed Bhim waiting till many of his Kaurav brothers got on trees to pluck the mangoes and wickedly Bhim would use his brute strength to shake the trees so that Duryodhan's brothers fell from them and broke their bones, with Bhim laughing uproariously at the spectacle. He had then tried to poison Bhim and leave him to drown but fate intervened and he came back unharmed and mightier after this episode.

Worse was to follow when the elders at the royal court made a decision to declare Yudhishthir as the Crown Prince and the heir apparent to the throne of Hastinapur and that's when he planned the House of Lac at Varnavrat. Here too, destiny had other things in store for him. The Pandavs returned to Hastinapur unharmed, on the way bringing for themselves a beautiful wife - Draupadi. The kingdom was then bifurcated into half, Pandavs were given Khandavaprastha and Kauravs retained Hastinapur.

As the king of Indraprastha, under the guidance of Krishna, Yudhishthir performed the Rajsuya Yagna at a magnificent ceremony in the presence of all the princes who had sworn allegiance to Yudhisthir's sovereignty. The Pandavs had all but transformed the barren, infertile land (Khandavaprastha) given to them into a prosperous city (Indraprastha) replete with architectural wonders, riches of trade and commerce. Duryodhan, one of the invitees, seethed with searing envy as his eyes took in all the splendour around him. He found a like-minded individual in Shishupal who hated Krishna as much or even more than Duryodhan hated Pandavs and they hatched a conspiracy to ruin the Rajsuya Yagna ceremony completely and Duryodhan promised to protect Shishupal if harm came his way. Shishupal thus egged on, hurled the worst invectives at Bhishma, Draupadi, and Krishna until Krishna used his Sudharshan Chakra and beheaded Shishupal on the spot.

Mayhem broke out at this, since Duryodhan realised that Shishupal had paid with his life and he had been unable to protect Shishupal. He immediately challenged Krishna to a duel and Karna and Dushasan who had accompanied Duryodhan also drew out their weapons. Bhishma and Vidur used their presence of mind and reigned in Duryodhan but the damage was done. Drawing out weapons against the crowned monarch in a Rajsuya Yagna was an offence punishable with death penalty and Yudhishthir struggled with a befitting punishment that would assert his sovereignty to the present kings and yet, not hurt Duryodhan's parents – Dhritrashtra and Gandhari – whom he held in highest esteem.

Draupadi then stepped in and suggested that a befitting punishment would be to divest all three offending warriors of their weapons (Shastraharan) and issue an order forbidding them to ever carry weapons within Indraprastha's territory! As per the mores of those days, for any warrior, this was a fate worse than death. Indeed Karn actually requested that he be given the death penalty (which had Kunti quite alarmed) rather than be subjected to such humiliation. Yudhishthir accepted Draupadi's suggestion and immediately issued such an order. The three warriors had to return to Hastinapur shorn of their weapons, reeling under abject humiliation!

Before they could return home, also happened the unfortunate incident of Duryodhan, blinded as he was by rage and shame, falling into an artificial waterbody, mistaking it to be terra firma, and the famous words attributed to Draupadi "Are the sons of blind, blind too?" History is divided on whether it was actually Draupadi who said it or her hand maiden and Draupadi had merely smiled at the mockery, but the damage was done. Duryodhan always held it against her, and waited for his revenge.

When the opportunity presented itself, he ordered the dishonour and disrobing of Draupadi not just because of an unfortunate remark but because she had ordered his "*Shastraharan*" long before he had ordered her "*Vastraharan*" (Disrobing.)

30. Duryodhan's Defence

As I see posterity maligning me as the proverbial black sheep,
Why doesn't anybody see the wounds on my psyche so deep?
At every occasion, rejected, humiliated, oh, so grievously slighted,
Advised to be killed at birth, accursed with a destiny so blighted!

How dare those vagabonds from the forest come and usurp my throne?
My father though sightless was the custodian king and I, his first born!
And whether it was Bhim's poisoning or the House of Lac burning away,
I had to get the Pandavs out of the way so I could be king one day!

As for the disrobing of Draupadi, supposedly my worst crime,
My soul still stands seared by the anguish and trauma of the time,
When Draupadi, in the full assembly of kings, divested me of my weapon,
Revenge was sweet when dragged and disrobed, she suffered naked humiliation!

Provoked to the extreme, vendetta has scripted my entire life's story,
Posterity will never know this, since it is always the victor who writes history!

Miscellaneous

A Leaf from Buddha's Book

Prologue

Among Buddha's various stories that I heard in my childhood, the story on which this poem is based, resonated with me the most. This seemed such a simple way to save yourself from unhappiness inflicted by others on your psyche. If you simply decline to accept every unhappy word, miserable act flung at you, it remains with the giver, after all it can hurt you only if you have accepted it and given it a place in your heart/ mind. And yet, over the years, we store every unpleasant memory, allow it to fester, sometimes plan elaborate revenge mechanisms around it, little knowing that anger is the acid that harms the container. This simple master key to my mind is even more superior in philosophy and simpler to practice than forgive and forget, which also we are taught with equal earnestness. Even to forgive, we would have allowed the hurt to enter our conscience, dwell on it, given it time and importance, and then, chosen to let go.

But had we rejected the hurt when it was inflicted on our psyche, we would have spared ourselves all the associated trauma arising out of that injury.

The beauty with all of Buddha's teachings through his stories is the simplicity of the most profound philosophies unravelling deep mysteries of our existence through simple day-to-day examples.

Whether you consider the story of Siddharth (Gautam Buddha) saving the bird felled down by Devdutt (his cousin) by an arrow and then both brothers staking a claim over the bird and the judge asking the bird to choose his master – the underlying philosophy is so simple – a living being will always choose his saviour over his predator and the lesson it imparts in kindness and compassion is profound without being preachy.

Or you consider the story of a distraught woman coming to Buddha with the corpse of her son and requesting him to bring life into the corpse again because she could not bear to see her son die – nay, not requesting him but challenging him that if he was indeed God (as everyone around him claimed he was) he should be able to do it. All Buddha did at that point of time was to ask her to get him some water which he needed to sprinkle over the child, but the water had to be obtained from a house of that village which had never seen death!

31. A Leaf from Buddha's Book...

Disciple

He is flinging curses and waste at you, now for a while;
And yet, you, unaffected, bless him with the same serene smile,
Everyday when you pass his house, he creates this small furore,
I shall fight him tomorrow, I cannot see you insulted anymore!

Buddha

What the world gives you, misery or happiness, is not in your control,
But your reaction to it, is the choice exercised by your soul!
If you choose not to accept what is given, it remains with the giver,
You maintain your inner peace and composure with simple declinature!

If he wants to anger me and I rise to his provocation,
I have relinquished my control to his evil intention,
We owe it to our psyche to disallow negativity and fill it with virtue,
And thus, we shall attain a mature mind and a soul pure and true.

Learning, meditation, renunciation, God allows you various ways,
And intends that we reach that exalted state of being happy always!

Bizarre Boons

Prologue

Hinduism treats the word GOD as an acronym of Generator, Operator, and Destroyer, thus accommodating the triumvirate of Brahma (The Generator), Vishnu (The Operator), and Shiv (The Destroyer) respectively in one small word of infinite import. So to Brahma goes the credit of creation, and whenever you see what in popular parlance are called Acts of God that is all destructive natural phenomena such as an earthquake, tsunami, flood, that God is definitely Shiv, the God of destruction. But the most difficult task undoubtedly rests on Vishnu's shoulders, the burden of running this world!

This sonnet of mine is a departure from practice, it is an *imaginary* conversation between a very hurt and fatigued Vishnu, who has the responsibility of administration of this universe, and he very justifiably thinks that his friends, Shiv and Brahma, well-meaning though they are, keep creating impediments for him, chiefly by granting all kinds of impossible boons to whoever appeases them.

Almost all my research has borne out this startling discovery that every Asura has always prayed to Brahma or Mahadev (also known as Ashutosh, literally meaning easily pleased) and obtained these bizarre boons. And it falls onto Vishnu to devise ways and means of destroying these demons without disrespecting the sanctity of those boons, regardless of how illogical they were in the first place.

Readers familiar with ancient history will easily identify the various boons granted by an easy-to- please

Shiv or Brahma – Ravan was granted the boon that no Sur (Dev) or Asura, demon, yaksha or any celestial being could kill him. But the icing on the cake in this particular aspect is definitely taken by Shiv! Shiv, Bholenath (guileless) that he was, had granted a boon to Bhasmasur, that whoever/ whatever Bhasmasur places his hand on would be burnt to ashes, without realizing that Bhasmasur with his newly granted boon and newly inculcated arrogance would want to test it on Shiv himself. Shiv was running for cover and sought Vishnu's help, who immediately transformed himself into Mohini (the most charming) and presented herself before Bhasmasur. Bhasmasur who had never before seen such an alluring maiden, was so besotted with her that he completely forgot his quest for Shiv and asked for her hand in marriage. Mohini agreed with a precondition, that in their dance together, if he could match her step for step, she would gladly marry him. Thus follows an elaborate dance ritual between Mohini and Bhasmasur, which is brought to an abrupt end, because in one of her poses, Mohini places her hand on her head, Bhasmasur emulates her and burns himself to ashes!

The poem starts with a dash of subtle humour when Vishnu reminds Shiv and Brahma of their boons and how he has had to devise and contrive various ways to restore order and maintain the universe and ends on a very sobering note in the response of Brahma and Mahadev to Vishnu.

32. Bizarre Boons

Vishnu to Shiv and Brahma
Mahadev, do think twice before granting the bizarre boons you give,
Thank Mohini, else the last one to Bhasmasura was pretty self- destructive!
Brahma, your boons of near immortality are also convoluted to say the least,
I have had to take strange avatars, sometimes as half man, half beast!

Once, my wife was kidnapped, and I had to lead an army of monkeys,
And yet in another, I was born in jail and had to plot my own release!
No wonder nobody appeases me, I just appear, smile and bless,
Instead of granting bizarre boons which always create an unholy mess!

Shiv and Brahma suitably chastised
No more shall we put you through such ordeals, my friend,
Though in Kaliyug, all your troubles must have come to an end.
Spirituality is lost, here man is a slave to machines and money,
His life is bereft of prayer and penance, peace and harmony.

There are no more deserving devotees, We have turned to stone,
Watching helplessly, as man creates destruction all alone!

www.ingramcontent.com/pod-product-compliance
Lightning Source LLC
Chambersburg PA
CBHW051057130726
48008CB00008B/36